RACING *Toward* RECOVERY

The Extraordinary Story of Iditarod Musher Mike Williams Sr.

By MIKE WILLIAMS SR. and LEW FREEDMAN

ALASKA
NORTHWEST
BOOKS®

Library of Congress Cataloging-in-Publication Data

Williams, Mike, 1952-
   Racing toward recovery : the extraordinary story of Iditarod Musher Mike Williams Sr. / by Mike Williams and Lew Freedman.
       pages cm
   ISBN 978-1-941821-44-2 (pbk. : alk. paper) 1. Williams, Mike, 1952-
2. Recovering alcoholics—Alaska—Biography. 3. Alaska Natives—Biography.
4. Iditarod (Alaska)—History. I. Freedman, Lew. II. Title.
   HV5293.W544A3 2015
   362.292092—dc23
   [B]
                              2014034748

Also available in e-book (978-1-941-821-67-1) and hardbound (978-1-941-821-77-0) formats.

Design by Vicki Knapton

Published by Alaska Northwest Books®
An imprint of

GRAPHIC ARTS
BOOKS®
P.O. Box 56118
Portland, Oregon 97238-6118
503-254-5591
www.graphicartsbooks.com

ABOUT THE AUTHORS

Mike Williams Sr. is a resident of the village of Akiak in Alaska. He is a longtime competitor in the Iditarod Trail Sled Dog Race, a leading figure in the Sobriety Movement for Alaska Natives, and an activist for improved living conditions for Natives in the Alaska Bush.

Lew Freedman is a veteran journalist and author who lived in Alaska for seventeen years and is the author of numerous books on dog mushing and stories from Alaska.

FOREWORDS

I have known Mike Williams since 1976 when I lived in Bethel. I knew Mike, his brother Walter, who was a really good sprint musher, the best of the best, and I knew his father Tim, who was a fisherman. I moved to Bethel to work for Alaska Fish and Game and everybody fished for salmon for their dogs.

When I first knew Mike, he and his brothers, and just about everyone else in the Bethel area, were subsistence fishermen. Mike and his brothers had a substance abuse problem. It is hard to watch people you really like self-destructing. It was just so sad. So it is incredible what Mike has overcome in his life.

Mike would come from Akiak and stay with me and my husband, Mike, in Bethel. So did his brothers. We loved to have them, but we were so worried about them. Once, I remember somebody going out in the winter without a coat because he was drunk. We prayed they didn't freeze to death on their way home.

Mike's brothers all were lost due to problems with alcohol, but Mike overcame the problem. You have to really respect where that man has come from. He is a spiritual inspiration.

Dog mushing was a big part of the Williams brothers' lives. It brought them into the forefront of the community and gave them some success. The key for Mike being strong was in part due to dog mushing. He recognized the destruction facing his family. His faith in God was the only thing strong enough to change him. And his wife, Maggie, was driven to be successful. She has been incredibly strong for Mike.

The Iditarod became a big part of Mike's life, too. I always thought that dog mushing can be a real savior for rural Alaska. It gives Alaska Natives a closeness to their culture. I love to see it when Alaska Natives do well in the Iditarod. There is a realization they can be the best in the world. This is one thing that can help save the culture.

When Mike announced that he was going to carry signatures of Alaskans pledging sobriety along the trail to Nome during the Iditarod I was really proud of him. I knew Mike had made a big change in his life.

I think that the Iditarod can be a platform for more than a single year's race. It is an opportunity to connect with people everywhere. You can squander it or use it. Mike used it and built it so that he became known as the musher for sobriety. Doing well and being out there is admired in his culture, too.

Dog mushing and the Iditarod are so loved and respected in the villages. The people respect that you are regularly taking on the challenge of the thousand miles of the Iditarod. They understand the weather, the elements, and how hard it can be to be out there. The fact that you are in first place or fiftieth place, they don't care. They respect that you, that Mike, is tough enough to stay with it. Mike has been using his platform in the Iditarod to build something for his people.

Over the years Mike and I have done training runs together. I have been in Akiak and he has been in Willow. I spent the night at their house. Our families are close.

Mike can get a little bit radical at times and there can be differences of opinions over issues, but the person behind what Mike says is someone who is watching his Eskimo culture diminish. At one time Akiak was more of a metropolis than Bethel was. Mike knows of the days when things were really rolling. He remembers the times when there were only honey buckets instead of flush toilets in the Bush. He has worked to make sure his people retain their dignity.

He is right about so many things. Many of our people in Alaska live in more deplorable conditions than in other countries where we send foreign aid.

Mike Williams does what's good for his people. I think Mike is very sincere. He's passionate, and his passion shows that he has a great heart. His motivation is correct, that he wants to help people.

—DeeDee Jonrowe
Veteran Iditarod Trail Sled Dog Race musher

first met Mike Williams about thirty years ago. He introduced himself to me when I was coordinating an Elders conference in the Bethel region. He said he was interested in doing things to help his people. My wife, Amy, and I had fostered what had become known as the Sobriety Movement.

There was a blue ribbon commission to evaluate the problem of alcohol in Alaska's Native villages and it was concluded that Native leaders needed to take responsibility if they wanted to make meaningful change in the villages.

The first tangible action that was taken was that Native Alaskans discontinued the availability of alcohol at their meetings and functions. Mike was modeling the behavior he was advocating. We have spoken pretty regularly over the years about the problems created by alcohol in the Alaska Bush.

We talked over ideas and what could be done. Mike came from a family that was severely impacted by alcohol use. He lost all of his brothers to alcohol-related accidents and Mike drank, too, before he got sober and began raising awareness about sobriety and recovery issues.

As long as people are hurting there have to be people who are willing to step up and face the issue. Mike is willing to do that. It takes a special kind of stamina and commitment to do that and to keep doing that.

Mike told me he was going to gather signatures of Alaska Natives pledging their sobriety. And then he would carry all of the signatures to Nome during the Iditarod in his dogsled. I told him I was looking forward to his involvement. I thought, *This is great.* He stepped up again in his way.

Many people who used to drink share their stories and feelings, but Mike went beyond that. He took it to a much bigger audience. He has carried signatures in his sled many times because he believes in the Sobriety Movement. He is totally tenacious in that regard. He paid a price because of alcohol in his family. He experienced tragedy, as many people do. Sobriety is one part of the message of recovery.

Mike understands the level of effort and attention that is required to get people to pay attention to the problem of alcohol in the Bush. He knows and he has never quit. I can always totally rely on Mike if work is needed. He is just very well-known for his tenacity in helping people.

When you think about the lives of Alaska Natives getting better, you think about Mike. You think about the good that he does and there is lots of good.

—Doug Modig
 Alaska Sobriety Movement leader

INTRODUCTION

The first time I met Mike Williams he was bundled up in a parka standing in a pile of mushy snow a short distance from Fourth Avenue in Anchorage, Alaska, awaiting the start of the Iditarod Trail Sled Dog Race.

At the time I was the sports editor of the *Anchorage Daily News* and Mike was an entrant in the thousand-mile race between Alaska's largest city and the old Gold Rush town of Nome on the Bering Sea Coast.

I had written about the race and Mike had mushed in the race, but he was upping the ante. He had decided that to shed light on one of Alaska's greatest threats to the health and future of its Native people he would carry in his sled pages—pounds worth—of signatures of people who had pledged sobriety. A Yup'ik Eskimo, Mike saw how alcohol could devastate people as surely as if they had contracted a deadly flu.

It was a cause close to his heart because Mike was the last surviving brother in what had once been a large family. Only each of his brothers had succumbed to alcohol-related accidents, incidents, or illnesses. He recognized alcoholism as a disease with terrible consequences that had wrecked his family. It had also almost claimed him, but he had righted himself.

Through religion, loved ones, and sustained determination, Mike Williams shed his own dependence on alcohol. That would be enough of a victory for some people, but Mike committed to spending much of his time working for the welfare of Alaska Natives by involving himself with committees, commissions, and tribal government.

A somewhat roly-poly man of about 260 pounds with a mustache, a dry sense of humor, and a love of laughter, Mike is an engaging fellow to spend time with and yet he is also a very serious man concerned about the issues of the day and overlooked problems in the Alaska Bush. Besides working so hard behind the scenes in meetings, besides committing himself very publicly to matters of serious import, Mike also involved himself in what for many others is a full-time endeavor—long-distance dog mushing.

For some entering the Iditarod is a once-in-a-lifetime event. For others, racing in the most prestigious dog-mushing competition in the world annually is a career. Mike somehow managed to compete in the Iditarod year after year at the same time as he was flying around the state, traveling to Washington, D.C., and attending regional meetings in Seattle, or wherever his responsibilities took him.

This was no mean feat, not only because of the time required, but because Mike's home is Akiak, Alaska. This is no metropolitan hub. No roads lead to the community in Southwest Alaska. Travel is possible by water on the Kuskokwim River, when it is not frozen solid in winter, and if someone is in no hurry. Air travel is the only way to move around swiftly, but departing from Akiak most likely means flying in a four-seater plane, taking off from a gravel runway. Then a traveler transfers to a jet in Bethel about twenty-two miles away, transfers to a jet in Anchorage, and then onward via another jet to Seattle, perhaps Chicago, then possibly to Washington, D.C., a somewhat frequent destination for Mike.

This is a guy who has been known to acquire frequent dog-mushing miles and frequent flyer miles equally.

Akiak has a population of about 350 people, predominantly of Yup'ik Eskimo heritage. The bounty of the Kuskokwim River provides much of the fish to feed the people who rely heavily on the water and surrounding land, fishing and hunting, for subsistence. Akiak's history dates to 1880 when it was established as a small town for wintering purposes among those who spent summers along the Kuskokwim River. The community is surrounded by the river and trees and driving from one end to the other takes only minutes. A common method of travel is by four-wheeler.

One characteristic of Akiak—an important one for Mike Williams—is that it is a dry town. Possession of alcohol is banned. In some ways Akiak is more advanced than other small Alaska Bush villages. The local school is modern and impressive looking. There is a clinic. There is a modern water-treatment plant and septic system. Housing in Akiak, as it is in most Alaska villages where the temperatures are severe in winter, where the wind buffets the walls, and the snow piles high, is sturdy, with rougher exteriors and warmer interiors, both in temperature and living style.

Although he has an office in a government building, Mike's main office is his kitchen table. He has a laptop computer and a cell phone that connect him to the outside world and from a kitchen chair he conducts business of all manner, routinely speaking to people thousands of miles away each day.

Mike's dog lot is a few hundred yards away, down the block, really, but the Williams kennel is chiefly run by Mike Williams Jr. these days. Son Mike spent many of his formative years helping his father feed, raise, and train his huskies. Now, with Mike Sr. in his sixties, Mike Jr. is the main racer in the family. Currently, Mike Sr. spends time helping feed, raise, and train the dogs for his son's efforts.

Mike Sr., now gray-haired, has competed in the Iditarod fifteen times, the last time in 2013. He may be retired, but rarely is that a sure thing with the Iditarod. At the least he is on a break from the demanding race, investing more effort into cheering for Mike Jr., who has put together a superior record in a short time.

A member of the Alaska Native Community and the National Congress of American Indians, Williams is the father of five children and grandfather of many, the number increasing annually.

The more time I spent talking with Mike Williams the more I enjoyed his company and gained respect for his efforts to improve the lives of those in rural Alaska who have suffered with alcoholism, a high suicide rate, below-standard plumbing and other infrastructure that most Americans take for granted. Although he was never a top contender for the Iditarod title, only once breaking into the top twenty, Williams was a fixture in the race, and a competitor whom everyone cheered.

Once, he was the only Yup'ik Eskimo musher, a symbol to all Natives around the state. Many years he carried those signatures, focusing attention on a troubling, seemingly intractable problem. Williams gained national attention, being profiled by CNN and *Good Morning America*. *Sports Illustrated* has taken note of his achievements. Fellow Iditarod competitors have voted him the most inspirational musher.

Although he never came close to recouping the costs of what it took to pull together an Iditarod team from his prize money, Mike was always there, one of the most popular entrants. As the years passed Mike and I became friendlier and I realized even more what an extraordinary man he was.

Williams deserves to have his life story told, the hardships and difficulties overcome, his rise to Iditarod prominence as one of the race's key, admired individuals, and for the causes he symbolizes and fights for.

A unique person, one who hunts and fishes and mushes dogs, the same activities his ancestors participated in, Mike lives far from the mainstream of daily American life, four hundred miles from Anchorage, nearly two thousand miles north of Seattle. But he is also someone heavily dependent on a computer and a telephone.

Mike Williams is a man of many parts, a sports figure, a government figure, a leader of his people, a husband, a father, and a Native man with one foot firmly planted in the twenty-first century and another firmly planted in the roots of a culture that dates back 10,000 years in Alaska.

—Lew Freedman

CHAPTER 1

My family has been in the area of Akiak for about 10,000 years. Always. We've been here from time immemorial. My father's name was Timothy Williams. His father was Peter Williams. My father was a chief and Peter Williams was a chief of the tribes here, the Akiak Koliganek.

Koliganek, that's where we were in the beginning. There is a story about the reason why Akiak became Akiak. A couple raised a brown bear from a little cub. The brown bear grew up in the village of Koliganek, but wanted the couple to move across the Kuskokwim River. The word *Akiak* means "across."

The couple did not want to give up the bear so the couple moved across the river because the bear was getting too big and was dangerous to the community. So that's how Akiak became Akiak. The bear grew up to be an adult and nobody would harm that bear. Eventually the bear left the village of Akiak and when people went out hunting they recognized that bear and would never shoot it because it was part of their community, part of the family of Akiak.

The Williams name came from a family in Akiak. My great-grandmother Lena got married to Waska Williams, who was from the Yukon. The village was a small place and sometimes cousins fell in love with one another. One grandmother, Elizabeth Kawagley, fell in love with her first cousin Peter Williams, but because they were too close in the same family the only way they could get married was to go out into the Gulf of Alaska. My mother's name is Helena Lomack Williams. There are special rules if first cousins get married: they have to do it away from the community. They ended up going to Kodiak and from there they went out to the Gulf of Alaska and got married outside of the land and on the water. They were my grandparents.

I was actually born in a log cabin right next to the Kuskokwim River. It was our family home at that time that my dad built. He had some help, but he mostly built it himself. He got logs from upriver and hauled them to Akiak or he found other logs nearby. A lot of people did that in the 1950s and earlier. People built their own homes here. There was no housing authority and there were no houses around here like the modern kind you would see now. People just made them out of logs.

The house I was born in was about three hundred yards from where I live now. It is still there, I think, but it is underwater, because of soil erosion along the banks of the Kuskokwim River. The old house fell into the river. When I was born a woman named Edith Kawagley helped. She was a traditional midwife. She delivered the majority of the people in Akiak. She was a nurse and delivered all of the babies around here. I was born September 29, 1952, in Akiak, in that departed house.

The house was standing there until only a few years ago when it gave way into the river. It stood there for a long time really. Since then we have had more bank erosion. At one point we lost sixty feet and another time when there was flooding a couple of springs ago we lost thirty more feet through erosion. We had lots of flooding recently and that always takes some of the bank away.

I was one of eight children. There were six brothers and two sisters. Frank was the oldest. He was an avid hunter and fisherman, one of the best hunters and fishermen I have ever known and he, along with my dad, taught me most of the things that I know about hunting and fishing. I think Frank was the best hunter and fisherman in Akiak.

Frank was about ten years older than me and he also taught me about dogs and mushing. We always had dogs in my family, forever. Ted was the second oldest, then me, and Walter and Gerald, Timothy Williams Jr., and Fred. And those are the brothers. My two sisters are Cathy and Lena Sharon.

We grew up with a subsistence way of life, as our people had for thousands of years. We hunted and fished for our own food. It was always regulated by our Elders and our community by season. We didn't grow up on junk food, just the fish and game the land provided. We hunted for moose and caribou in the fall. We also hunted for rabbits. Really, anything with four legs, we would hunt. We trapped beaver, too. There were also black bears and grizzly around and porcupines. They're all here. The bears come through town. They raid our fish camps.

In the Kuskokwim River we fish for king salmon—*Chinook*—white fish, chum, sockeye, silver salmon, pike, sheefish, and in winter, pretty much starting in November, we fish through the ice for burbot and whitefish.

In the spring we pick greens from the ground, cook them, and put them away. Berry picking starts in the summer. There are salmon berries, blackberries, red berries, blueberries, and highbush red berries. I have been doing this since I was a child. All of it, hunting, fishing, trapping, and berry picking. We all did it—all of the boys—every year. Our lifestyle and our diet were dictated by the seasons. It is always all about what is available at what time. The land provides and the river provides. And we're always gathering for winter. That's been true my whole life.

For me I have always enjoyed most going out in the fall camping when we went moose hunting and caribou hunting. Moose and caribou hunting are the best. I started to go out on hunts when I was about seven years old and I started regularly hunting by the time I was ten. In the beginning I used a .22 rifle. The first species I ever hunted was migratory birds, ducks and geese. That's what I started off with and as I got older I hunted moose, caribou, and bear.

Part of the excitement in the spring was going to fish camp with the family when the birds migrated. It took a lot of prep time to go to camp. I liked establishing the camp and getting settled in, just being there. You have your tent, your sleeping gear, your stove, your food like flour, sugar, coffee, tea, and the utensils like the cooking pot. Camp was about fifteen to twenty miles from home.

We would start to set up camp in March and there was plenty of snow on the ground so we went by dog team. Then, in early April we would set up the tent. In the spring we trapped for muskrat. That was our cash cow. It took thirty-two muskrat to make a coat and that's what the fur buyers wanted. At the same time we hunted our migratory birds. We lived off the land in spring camp while we trapped.

Although we trapped furs and traded them for cash, essentially when I was growing up Akiak was a cashless society. We were basically living off the land. In the summer we could commercial fish closer to Bethel and turn in the fish for cash. Some people spent their summers working at canneries in Bristol Bay. And some guys would go to fight fires in the Interior for a summer job. They were smokejumpers.

But trapping was important. Some of it was muskrat, but in the fall we trapped for mink and other fur-bearing animals. Trapping beaver and turning in beaver pelts was good business. If you got cash you could use it for ammunition for your rifle and for supplies like flour, sugar, coffee, and other necessities.

Usually we bought things like that in Bethel, but we also had mail-order catalogs around the house like Sears Roebuck and Montgomery Ward. That was the American way, wasn't it? Every year my mom ordered things for us before school started. We didn't get our winter coats from a catalog. A lot of our protective clothing was handmade. We had mukluks for our feet that were made from sealskins or fur-bearing animals. My mom made us parkas. The coats came from fur-bearing animals.

Fall camp was set up in September. It was before it snowed. Camp could be anywhere from five miles to a hundred miles away from home. We went by boat along the Kuskokwim River for those camps. Somebody said that was pretty much like the lifestyle in the West in the United States in the 1800s. That's probably true. I'm not sure how much people in the Lower 48 of the US know about our lifestyle now, whether they would believe it or not if they heard about it. I don't know if they understand it. They live near big grocery stores that have everything. We provide our own food—most of it—still today. I think we need to educate them as much as we can about that way of life. It's not a chosen lifestyle just for the heck of it, it is life. The lifestyle we adopted long ago was practiced from generation to generation and has been going on from time immemorial.

The place we live also dictates what we do. We live off the land, but the land is alongside the river. We do not live near a highway that can take you anywhere to go shopping. The lifestyle and the place come together. This is a big part of me. This is where I grew up. That's how my dad and my grandparents lived and it goes way back. Each generation is taught the same way of doing things.

Akiak is a small place with only about 350 people. A lot of the people are interrelated as cousins because in the beginning there were four Williams sisters who were here and got married. Not very many people have moved out, but they always stayed here and existed here. So we're interrelated to a large extent and we have been helping each other survive over the years. It is not a transient community. The door is always open in my house and my relatives come in and out and they stop by for lunch and eat whatever we have.

In a small community like this everybody helps everybody. If we see people that need help we give them help. If they need food or they need water, if they need shelter, we've been able to prevent problems in our community for a long time. There is a sense of family, a sense of being together and supporting each other.

People might be surprised by this, but in summer it can get up to eighty or ninety degrees. Not every day, but it can. That would be June or July, not usually August. Temperature year-round averages about fifty degrees, so it is pretty cold in the winter. Winter comes early compared to what the calendar says in other places, but it used to come earlier. Over the last fifty years I think I have seen climate change. When I was young fall was in early September and by the end of September we would see the river freeze. Now it's like late October or mid-November.

I'd also say that about twenty or thirty years ago we used to see a lot more snow. We seem to be seeing less and less. Still, our winter is much more winter than most people around the United States get, for sure. When it's really cold in Akiak it can be between minus sixty and minus seventy. It does get that cold, but we still have to do things. I've got to put on my parka and go out and feed the dogs.

I know when the average person in the Lower 48 hears those temperatures they shiver. They wonder how we could function and do anything at all. They ask how we put up with it, why don't we stay in the house. That's the way that people think.

You have to have good clothing and some good protection for the dogs. You have to be protected from the cold and the wind. But we just can't afford to stay home and not do anything. Maybe if it was for one day, but not more than that.

When it is that cold our snowmachines won't start. Before we had snowmachines when it was extremely cold, we went out by dog team. They didn't mind going out at any time. And they never broke down. Even when it was so cold we had to go out to chop wood and haul it. We went between five miles and twenty miles from home to chop spruce. It was very dry.

I was seven years old when I started going out with someone in the family to chop wood. Then I went on my own with my friend Willie Lake. In the winter we had a team of five to seven dogs and a saw. We went out, cut the wood, filled the sled, and came back. I learned about Alaska huskies from an early age. When we wanted to go visit someone in another village the dogs were our mode of transportation, not snowmachines, at least not in the 1960s.

Snowmachines started showing up in the 1970s and that's when our life changed. Everybody in Akiak had dogs then, but after the snowmachine arrived they got rid of a lot of them. There are probably four families in Akiak now that still have dogs. We have a kennel of about fifty or sixty dogs. We have always, consistently, had dogs. My family has had dogs as far back as I can remember. Now it is me and Mike Jr.

Another chore that I had as a kid was to haul water. It came from the Kuskokwim River. My dad made a kind of well and we'd pump out the well. We also got blocks of ice from the river and melted them.

When I was a kid sprint mushing was a big thing in the Alaska villages. Everyone had races and it was the biggest thing to do in the winter, the best entertainment. There were a lot of winter carnivals—there are still some—and the featured event was always the dog races. They included kids, so when I was a little boy my first races were with three or five dogs in the villages. Akiak held them, but there were races all over the area in Bethel, Tuluksak, Kwethluk, everywhere. They took turns each winter.

CHAPTER 2

When I think back to early in my life I think of a lot of good times. One thing we did when it was break-up and the ice was melting was go swimming. It wasn't in the river, but in these giant puddles. I remember playing with friends every day, going hunting and fishing. Sometimes we chopped wood for the Elders and just hung out.

John Egoak was one of my best friends. He was the oldest one and he knew more things. We were actually three best friends, me, John, and Willie Lake, but John showed us things. He showed how they made the log cabins and how they filled in the cracks with moss from the tundra. He also showed us how he built his strength. He was really strong. He teased us, I guess. He took some of the moss and rolled it up into a cigarette. Then he lit it up and smoked that moss and said, "This is the reason I am so strong. What I am smoking makes me strong. If you smoke this, you will become strong, too." And we believed him. So we tried it and coughed like heck. It did not make us strong. We got very sick.

John has passed away. Willie works in Bethel. He's an optician who has been doing that for over thirty years.

When I started elementary school in grades kindergarten through fourth grade, we had a teaching staff from the Bureau of Indian Affairs. It was a two-room school, one for those grades and one for fifth grade through eighth grade. We had another room for that. There was one teacher in each room for all of the grades. It was an interesting setup. I think there were about ten kids in my class all of the way from kindergarten through eighth grade. That was my group.

One boy, John Jasper, was born a day after I was, so we basically grew up together and I became really close with his parents. John grew up in a traditional Eskimo family where his parents did not speak any English and he grew up in a traditional way. I stopped by his house every day to walk to school with him. He was sort of a quiet guy, but he was very bright. John was not a very big person physically. He could think things through and he was very smart.

I always cherished his parents, especially his mother. She would tell us the rules for living and to have a strong faith in God. His dad was a quiet guy, Willie Jasper. He was always driving his dog team. He also taught us about how to set fish traps under the ice in November about four or five miles from Akiak. He was an expert and my brother Walter and I would hang around with him. He would hitch up his dogs and we would hitch up our dogs and we took off after him. The fish traps were three feet by three feet by ten feet in size. The real name of the fish we trapped is burbot, but we called them lush fish. I don't know why.

I learned how to hunt by going out with my dad and brother Frankie. They were hunting for moose and took me along. They always got their moose. Mostly I was traveling with them. We had a canoe that we used on the lakes when we were trapping muskrat and hunting ducks at the same time.

From the beginning I was a good shot with a rifle. I had to be. You have to learn and you have to gain experience, but I was a good shot. Maybe it was because Frankie taught me. He was the best shot. When I was a young boy the best part of it all was being able to go out on a hunt with my father and older brother. It was a good feeling that they trusted me to come along. It meant a lot. They made me confident in myself. Doing those things built confidence. I learned how to set up camps and about survival. Once I knew how to hunt I knew I was going to be able to survive because I would have something to eat. It was a case of knowing that I could always go back home with something.

It was also a good feeling to understand that they were preparing me to survive on my own and teaching me how to provide for the family. My dad was with me more than anything on these trips, especially on fishing trips. He showed me how to fish, where to fish, and what the best times of day were to fish. It was the same with hunting. You had to get up really early when we went hunting, about four o'clock in the morning. Boy, it was hard to get up. A lot of kids don't like that, but I always woke up. The smell of coffee was good and maybe we ate pound cakes.

I had learned about those lush fish traps with Willie Jasper. He showed us exactly how to do it, how to set it, how to make the trap. That was a big help to me and Walter. The Jasper family also came to the same spring camp as we did. We always seemed to be together in spring camp and fish camp. I spent a lot of time with Nelson Jasper, John's oldest brother, who was a captain in the National Guard. He was an outgoing guy and he taught me a lot, too. He taught me how to fix small engines and we did some boatbuilding, as well. Nelson and my brother Frank were the best of friends. They did a lot of hunting together and hung out a lot. That was one family that I really appreciated the guidance from, as well as my own.

Those lessons I learned as a boy are still important to me now. I think they rooted me in being independent and not dependent on anything or anybody else. They were teaching me to be able to take care of myself and confident in whatever I did. I have confidence in what I need to do and it came from those times. They also taught me that you had to work for what you needed. They had discipline. There was a sense of responsibility in providing for yourself and the family.

I come back to discipline. My father and Frankie had a lot of discipline. Not just to be able to get up in the morning, but to carry out all of their tasks in the right way. They were adapting to the environment and they took care of the fish and the meat. They took care of everything in providing food for the family.

Part of what I learned was to be respectful of the animals. They were our food, but in a way moose were presenting themselves to us to eat. Also part of the entire experience learning to hunt and to fish was sharing what you got. I was taught to share what you had, what you gather, and what you catch with others who needed food. That's what we did and that's what we do now. If we hunt a moose we share the meat. If we catch fish in the nets on the Kuskokwim River, we share the fish. There are always people who need food and there are Elders who fished and hunted for a lifetime who are no longer strong enough to work to get their food. It is our responsibility to make sure they have enough to eat.

That has always been the way of our people going back in time. The majority of the people in Akiak come from people who grew up in the Kuskokwim Mountains or Kilibuck Mountains. Maybe some were from as far away as Denali. When they hunted they covered great distances. They spread through areas like Rohn and Rainy Pass—which are now checkpoints on the Iditarod Trail Sled Dog Race. Going back, my grandfather and great-grandfather were long-distance travelers. They hunted as far away as Nikolai. They were traveling by dog team.

Our Native language is Yupiaq and we continue to speak it, in addition to English. We still speak Yupiaq at home a lot of the time. When I was six years old I started school at the Bureau of Indian Affairs school in Akiak. Our school was grades kindergarten through eighth grade, but we did not have a high school then. It was about 1958 when I started school and there were no high schools in small Alaska Bush villages at that time. If you wanted to continue your education you had to go somewhere else.

When I was fifteen I was shipped out to the Wrangell Institute. That was a Bureau of Indian Affairs boarding school in Wrangell, Alaska, in the southeast section of the state. They prepared us to go to either Mount Edgecumbe in Sitka or the Chemewa Indian School in Salem, Oregon. That was one of the hardest things we had to go through, being separated from our families if we wanted a high school education.

Everything about going to Wrangell was different from being in Akiak. It was a boarding school in another part of Alaska hundreds of miles away. We didn't hunt and fish. We lived with other Alaska Natives. Akiak was a cold, dry climate and Wrangell was a wet, milder climate. When I got there it felt like a prison. I had to go there. My parents had no other options for me other than to send me out. It was a trust obligation of the federal government to educate us and the goal was to assimilate Alaska Natives into the mainstream of United States life. It was about being acculturated. They wanted to do away with our culture and replace it with the everyday culture of the rest of the country. It was a necessary thing to do if you wanted an education. You were taken from your family and sent to this new place. That is why it was so important later to have schools built locally in rural Alaska. You could stay home and still get an education. You could still be with your family.

I was fifteen years old and I had spent my whole life in Akiak. I was in a close family with all of those brothers and sisters and I had to say good-bye to them. I had grown up hunting, fishing, and berry picking and gathering and then I was by myself in Wrangell. Not completely by myself, though, because there were other kids at the school from villages who were just like me, who were in the same situation.

When we got to Wrangell, though, right from the beginning our joke was that we had been sent to prison. This was all to thoroughly prepare us for high school somewhere else. It was the next level of our education. We had a good math teacher and a good language arts teacher. Something else they did at the Wrangell Institute was to show us how to use a telephone. In those days there weren't any telephones in the Alaska Bush, never mind cell phones. We didn't have landlines in the Bush. We didn't really know what a telephone looked like when we first got there.

Learning things was the good part, but there was a lot about being sent to Wrangell that was not much fun. Right away they gave us haircuts and cut our hair short, too. Then they sent us to showers to clean up. In the beginning it was all very unpleasant and a shock to us. We had to march around like soldiers, like little soldiers, divided into age groups and grade groups. We were supposed to march everywhere we went.

The worst thing about being in Wrangell was that we were not with our families. It was a completely different world. You are taken from a loving family with your mother, father, brothers, and sisters, doing things you have always done, to a completely different situation. You lived in a dormitory setting with running water and ate different food that was prepared differently from the way it was at home. We had to stand in line. We had to get haircuts and keep our hair short. The haircut was a big deal. We hated getting our hair cut and I didn't like the haircut the way it looked.

They also inspected us. You had to get up at a certain time of day and make your bed. There were all these details and orders that we had to follow and if they weren't just right under the rules we got yelled at. We were yelled at all of the time. They would go, "You!" And it was do this, do that. Go to bed, be quiet. It was a completely different environment from Yup'ik home life. It was different and we didn't like it. What kept us boys going was that we had each other. We could talk to one another in Yupiaq, so we had our own language. We had each other and that helped us to survive.

Really, from the time we first started school, the United States government, through the Bureau of Indian Affairs, worked to wipe out our culture. At home we spoke Yupiaq, but when I entered elementary school in the BIA school I started learning to speak in English. It was not a bad thing to learn English, but they would not allow us to speak our native language at all. When we were not in the classroom, though, we spoke Yupiaq with our friends. We just kept speaking it when no one was around to tell us not to do it.

The goal was to make us into good little American boys. They had an assimilation process and that's what they stuck to doing. We had to learn about Dick and Jane and that nuclear family even if our lives were completely different from the lives that Dick and Jane led. They were always clean—they didn't get dirty from working outside—and they had a nice car. We didn't have cars in Akiak. The teachers presented this to us as the ideal, the way we should be and the way we should aspire to be.

The same thing continued at the Wrangell Institute for a year. We looked at pictures of Dick and Jane and we knew we didn't look like that or act like that. I'll never forget an instructor teaching us what a "curb" was. We didn't have paved streets in Akiak, never mind sidewalks with a curb. It seemed like a long year. I didn't really want to be there. It was not something I had expected to do. There was some value in the curriculum. The math skills and working on the English language, I got something out of those. They helped me. That was definitely preparation for secondary education.

But there were also long periods of homesickness. You cried. I was a teenager in 1968. My family didn't have a telephone in Akiak so I couldn't talk to them. We never spoke. We communicated by letter only. We were completely cut off except by letter. They were far away. Wrangell was a hard place to be for a lot of kids and we lost out on parenting. They deprived us of our loving parents and our way of life. I missed hunting and fishing. It was different to have to follow all of those rules and regulations in boarding school and having to march around.

There were also kids there that were much younger than us. They went to school there because their village did not have a school that went up to eighth grade. So you had some really small kids there, eight, nine years old, from villages. I think a lot of those kids could not handle it being away from their homes and they lost it afterwards. They were much younger than us and they had been removed from their homes.

As an adult I understand what they were thinking. They were trying to provide some sort of education, but not in our own culture. I think they could have afforded us the same education in our communities and eventually that's what happened. I believe the federal government had the responsibility to provide education in our communities and it did not do that. They just provided K through eight instead of K through twelve. They should have provided the whole thing without sending us to boarding schools. I think we're still living with the damage done to some of those individuals. Later, when Alaska got oil money and there were lawsuits, schools were built in all of the villages to provide K through twelve as it should have been from the beginning.

That form of schooling out of town changed us from having a strong family unit to breaking us down. Then we had to adjust when we came back to villages. It was very difficult for us. Also, as adults that had children, they had a tough time raising them in the proper Yup'ik way, in the traditional way, as had been done in the past.

One thing I did like about being at Wrangell was the sports teams. That was good. I really enjoyed getting involved. I played basketball and I participated in track and field and long-distance running. For me, that was a relief from the rest of the routine.

When the school year ended in the spring I went home and it was so good to be back. My family was going to spring camp for hunting and I went almost directly from Wrangell to spring camp. That was so nice. It was a good homecoming. It was always good to be back with my brothers and sisters.

Looking back I can see that not everything was wrong at Wrangell. The curriculum, the schooling, was OK, was even good in some respects. But the marching around was silly and it was a loss not to be with our parents at a young age when you need your parents. We didn't have that. We resented that somewhat and we would be angry at members of the staff that we felt treated us badly. I think I've gotten over it, but I still feel some resentment about the way it was all done. There were kids who went to school there and later hurt themselves, committing suicide, or drank themselves to death.

Sometimes I think a majority of those kids from Wrangell did not succeed in life. Or maybe they succeeded in a limited way. But I think damage was done. There was some healing. Going to Wrangell that year affected my life. My old friend Willie and I still talk about it sometimes. We say, "It's get-up time. It's detail time." We make those sarcastic comments. We remember those days.

CHAPTER 3

That was a very good homecoming after Wrangell. I got back to doing what I had always been doing with my family. But after the summer passed I was in the same situation again. If I wanted to continue my education, go on and attend high school, there were not many choices. There was no high school in Akiak.

I ended up attending Chemawa Indian School in Oregon. The year in Wrangell was just preparation for four years of high school, starting with the ninth grade. Part of me still wanted to stay home, but I was also excited a bit by going outside of Alaska and seeing another state. This was another boarding school. Going to live out of state seemed different from going to another school in another part of Alaska. I flew into Seattle and then took a bus to Salem, Oregon.

Chemawa was a lot like Wrangell, but it was bigger. There were three dormitories there, Brewer Hall, McNary Hall, and Mitchell Hall. But they had the same kind of rules. It was the same thing as at Wrangell. We had to get up in the morning at a certain time, do this, do that. But the kids were more independent because we were older than we had been at Wrangell. I arrived for high school in the fall of 1969.

Sports had been a high point for me at Wrangell so I wanted to continue playing sports at Chemawa. One big difference was that they had a football team. That was one thing I wanted to try and I did. The mix of people at the school was interesting. There were people at Chemawa from all over Alaska, from Point Barrow, Southeast, the Interior, and also Indian tribes from the Northwest. There were kids there from the Navajo nation.

There were a whole bunch of tribal kids in the student body and we were all curious about football. Nobody had really played, but we had seen games on television and wanted to try it. There were Eskimos from everywhere who signed up. On the first day we were in the locker room and the coach came in and gave as all of the equipment to put on. He said to put it on and go out and play football. We had to figure out how to put the equipment on by ourselves.

Nobody told us how to do it. If you have ever seen all of the pads that go on under the uniform you will know it is not as easy as it sounds to figure out what goes where. We put the hip pads on and then we tried to figure where the piece that was the tail guard went. We wondered what it was for. Was it for our backsides? Or was it to protect our private parts? We didn't know. We figured that it was to protect our private parts in case we got hit by a helmet on a play. So we agreed on how to put the pads on and ran out to practice. It was very uncomfortable. You had all of these Eskimo kids running around on the football field being very uncomfortable because we had the pads on backwards. Ouch.

We couldn't move very well and we were grimacing and frowning. All of the coaches looked at us and they were smiling, then they were snickering and then they were laughing. We made the adjustments quickly.

At that time my body was built very differently than it is built now. I was about five-foot-seven inches tall and weighed around 150 pounds. I was also a pretty fast runner, so because of my speed they made me a running back. I was a sprinter back then. Mostly I played positions for a smaller, fast guy. I was a running back throughout my football career and I also returned punts and kickoffs. On defense I was a linebacker. Everybody played offense and defense both at the time. I loved playing football. I really loved it. Our team was the Chemawa Braves.

I was 150 pounds when I first went out for football, but I grew. I got to be 160 pounds and then 170 pounds. I am big-boned, so I had the body frame to handle more weight. I was a fast runner, but I also had some strength from the lifestyle I led in the outdoors at home in Akiak, hunting and fishing and chopping wood.

We didn't have a lot of size on our team. I think our linemen averaged like 180 or 190 pounds. We played a lot against white schools that had guys that were six-foot-two hulks who weighed 250 pounds. I think our tallest guy was six-foot-one. We were smaller, but we were fast. Our teams weren't bad.

Our team had a wonderful coach. His name is Kugie Louis. He was the football coach and the track coach. I got the best coaching. He built our stamina and toughness. He was always big on fundamentals. He stressed knowing the fundamentals of the game and always being prepared to play. He talked about us being prepared to run and being prepared to have your body withstand pain. He was the best coach I ever had.

In high school I played football, basketball, and competed on the track team. I was the captain of the freshman team in basketball in ninth grade. As a sophomore I played on the junior varsity and the varsity. My junior year I was cocaptain of the basketball team.

As a member of the track team I ran the 100-yard dash and the 220. I also did some low hurdles and high hurdles. My best event was probably the 100-yard dash. My best time was 10.5 seconds. My best 220 time was under 23 seconds. I wasn't slow.

The Chemawa school was a lot like being at Wrangell in that I was living away from home again and a lot of the program was aimed at acculturation. They still wanted to strip away our culture, I think, but it was a little bit more liberal in that we were allowed traditional dances. The Navajos did some Indian dancing and the Northwest tribes did their dances. They were good dancers, too.

They did tell us that our goal should be to go to college. Academics were stressed and I think they had a pretty good academic program. I was a pretty good student overall. I had good enough grades to make it to the honor roll. I was a good athlete who was good in sports and that's how the other students knew me. I had not participated in student council or student government in any way, but at the end of my junior year I decided to run for student body president. I won.

That was the first time I had ever been involved in student government and I didn't know what I was getting into. Suddenly, I was into politics and I got interested in that. From there I dropped sports and focused on student government. During the summer after my junior year I went to a training program in the central part of Missouri at Westmont College to learn more about it.

I was given the opportunity to spend three weeks at this small, liberal arts college not far from St. Louis. There were kids there from all over the United States. It was an intensive program where I learned how to conduct meetings and understand Roberts Rules of Order, politics, and the issues of student governments. It was designed to help develop leadership and that's where I think I got all of the leadership skills I needed to carry out my presidential duties my senior year.

So I gave up sports for politics for my senior year. I could have done both, but I decided to focus more on academics and student government.

I think my four years in Oregon really helped shape me as a person. I broadened my horizons. I got a chance to play on sports teams. I became president of the student body and learned about political issues. That was a whole new area for me then. The school did ask quite a bit from its students. I got an exposure to the western way of life in the United States, and by that I mean western as in American as opposed to Native. But Chemawa also made us learn practical skills. We did our own banking and by that I mean that we started a student bank my senior year. We started other programs. One was like a junior entrepreneurship and we started a business selling hamburgers. The business was for fund-raising for the student body.

We started another program built around alcohol education. We had all heard for years from white people and from movies that there was an image of "the drunken Indian" out there in society. We started a program when I was school president to try and focus on changing that image of the drunken Indian. It was basically a counseling program for people with substance abuse problems, both for students and staff who needed help. I was only twenty years old at the time, but I recognized that my people had problems with alcohol that needed to be fixed.

One thing we worked on was alcohol awareness in terms of the harm it could do. I worked with a guy named Steve Labuff. We also started a campus patrol program to help people who were drunk and to prevent crime problems. We wanted our campus to be safe and to make sure people got home all right.

Part of the idea was also to improve the image of Alaska Natives and Indians by promoting heroes. Ira Hayes was one of the six Marines that worked to raise the flag on Iwo Jima during World War II in the famous photograph. He helped to raise that flag.

My father saw the future pretty well. Although he was very involved in preserving Native traditions he also knew that things were going to change. He told his children that we should get a good education and get as much schooling as we could. I think getting that western education was important. I remember my dad saying, "I think you guys need to go get your education and try your best in school because you're going to be dealing, negotiating for land. You're going to be negotiating your rights. You're going to be negotiating a lot of big issues that are going to come up."

He really knew what he was talking about on this subject. He said we should try to go to the best schools that have the best education and provide the best opportunities. "Try to get as much education as you can so you can protect what we have," he said. "We're going to be challenged for our way of life." His generation did not get a similar education and many could not read or write, nor could they understand these government policies that were popping up.

He was right. The Alaska Native Claims Settlement Act was implemented in 1971. The act was signed into law by President Richard Nixon and formalized land dispersal in Alaska to twelve Native corporations and 200 village corporations. A few years later the Alaska Pipeline opened and began pumping oil from the North Slope of Alaska not far from Barrow. Congress passed the Endangered Species Act in 1973 and that affected Alaska Natives' hunting and fishing prospects. The Molly Hootch Case resulted in a consent decree in 1976. That came from a lawsuit filed by Alaska teenagers that provided for more education in villages. New high schools were built all over. If that had become the policy a decade earlier I never would have had to go live in Wrangell or go to school in Oregon.

All of these huge issues affected rural Alaskans economically, in our subsistence lifestyle, and in the way we educated our children.

When I was a teenager going to Chemawa my father—and other Elders—said getting a white man's education was important, regardless of whether we liked it or not. They understood they had been passed by and missed out on getting a high school or college education and they wanted things to be better for their children and grandchildren. Their thinking was: You guys have to go. Go and try to get your degree because you are going to be dealing with these tough issues. It was important to my dad and my mom and the Elders for people like me to get that western education. They were concerned about the future and they had every right to be.

Even though I liked Chemawa more than Wrangell and I had some good experiences there, I was still homesick a lot. When I came home during the summers I got jobs either working in the canneries in Dillingham fish processing, or working as a firefighter. Alaska always had forest fires in the summer when it gets dry and lightning strikes. Most of the fires start that way. I got to see my family, but I had to work for money during the summer for my expenses at school.

In Akiak we could live from hunting and fishing and berry picking, but I needed cash in Oregon. My entire four-year high school experience was a lot like going to college for four years. My schedule was structured the same way. Go to school in the fall, come home in the spring and visit with the family briefly, and then go make some money to have at school. I couldn't really depend on my mom or my dad for money because they didn't have any. My dad was a businessman by then, though, running a grocery store. The store was called the Tim Williams Store. My grandfather Peter Williams had his own store that was just down the road from where my dog yard is now.

My grandfather was a very good businessman. He traveled to Seattle, to San Francisco, to Japan as part of his business work. I don't know how he did it with his limited education, but I believe he did very well as a businessman. After my grandfather Peter died, his brother Joe took over. He ended up selling it to a Native cooperative, so we didn't have the store in the family anymore. Then my father started his store. I never worked in the store. My father pretty much took care of the store on his own. I wasn't that interested in working there. I worked, but I did other things that interested me more.

When I became the president of the student body at Chemawa it opened a lot of doors to opportunities and experiences. That afforded me the chance to visit with the Yakima Indian nation and to travel to the Navaho nation. The goal was to visit tribes and learn how they operated. That was part of becoming a leader and I learned quite a bit. Looking over the tribes had a big influence on me. It was a good political education and taught me lessons about leadership.

By being elected president of the student body I got an entirely other kind of education at Chemawa. I learned a lot of politics and I learned about other Native tribes and cultures. My advisor, Clement Azure, was the one who suggested the training prior to my term as president. He was one of the best student advisors.

Up until then I didn't know how to run a meeting or carry out the directions or rules that the student body made or the student council passed. I'd say the school benefitted from me attending that program in Missouri. I learned about much more than overseeing meetings. I learned how to do something. For me alcohol was already an issue to be looked at. When I traveled I heard that "drunken Indian" phrase a lot. I heard people say that if they just looked at the way Indians were portrayed in the media, they were all drunks. The portrayal in many places, certainly the movies, did show all Indians as drunks who didn't know what they were doing. The image was that they are all killing themselves and that they're always drunk.

At that time the activists Russell Means and Dennis Banks were making speeches and they came to our school. They talked about the American Indian Movement and sovereignty. They really got me thinking when they talked about the history of how the federal government had treated Indians and Alaska Natives. They said, "It's not right. We need to change that. We need to take our land back. We need to take our rights back. We've lost them so far." What was interesting was that the United States was involved in a war in South Vietnam at the time and they seemed to be making waves.

I was wondering, *Gee, how come these guys are saying that?* I was strongly affected by it. Most of the Native people I knew were not like that. Our people were healthy. They weren't like that stereotype. I thought, *We're better than that.* I also did a lot of reading, books like *Custer Died for Your Sins*, and read about the Wounded Knee Movement.

Russell Means and Dennis Banks made a big impression on me and they were right. American Indians had lost their land and they wanted to reclaim some of that land. The American government broke every promise it made to Indians. It broke every treaty.

My senior year was a turning point for my life. It raised my consciousness. I became much more socially aware. I had liked playing sports and I had fun doing it. When I made the change to becoming student body president my last year in high school that one thing became a big part of my life. That time period led me to the rest of my life. Yes, I do like dog mushing and remain involved in that sport, but becoming student body president and having those experiences helped me for the next thirty or forty years.

That year I threw myself full blast into politics and government and issues. I gained so much awareness. It was never the same for me after that.

CHAPTER 4

What I learned during that year, after being student body president, after starting those programs, after the reading I did, and after hearing Russell Means and Dennis Banks, was that if I invested my time in good programs I could change attitudes. I wanted to change the idea that drunken Indians were no good. I wanted to overcome that image. We did a good job of it there at school, but I wanted to continue it.

To me it meant that if I am a drunken Indian I am a loser. I wanted us to feel good about who we were and who we were as Eskimos and Alaska Natives. That year was empowering.

I graduated from high school at Chemawa in 1972 and at that point I wanted to become a coach. I wanted to coach a football team, a basketball team, or become a physical education teacher. That was my goal. That was my thinking. I thought I could use my athletic background in a career and do good things for young people, as well. I wanted to work with young people and help others.

My plan was to attend Oregon College of Education in Monmouth, Oregon, which is now Western Oregon University. I wanted to earn a degree in education so I could teach and coach at the high school level. I thought I would be able to play football there, too, which I wanted to do. I wanted to get back to football. My junior year in high school I had made All-State. But I knew I could still play at that level.

Only one thing happened. I got drafted right after high school. By then my brother Ted was in the army. He had been drafted and sent to Vietnam. I was very close to Frank because he tutored me so much when I was a boy. He influenced me in everything, hunting, fishing, and everything else. He was a mentor. But Ted was, too.

Ted was another tough kid. He was the one who taught me how to box. We made boxing gloves out of socks and were hitting each other. We grew up boxing a lot. My mom got tired of us using the socks that way so we bought some boxing gloves from one of the catalogs.

We got pretty serious about the boxing and one time I punched Ted really hard and loosened his teeth. He fell backwards and was kind of knocked out for a while. Even if you are boxing with your brother you have to protect yourself at all times—that's the first rule of boxing—and you've got to fight to the max or you'll get it. You don't back down on anybody. You fight. You don't let them beat you. You beat them. That really helped me.

Only we were doing all of this fighting in the house. My mother was not thrilled about it at all. Later, Ted and I were in high school together. He was two grades ahead of me. He had some wonderful friends from Hydaburg in Southeast and we always had good friends from Akiak with us in high school. We stuck together and we stuck up for each other, so nobody bothered us. We defended ourselves if we had to and we kicked butt in high school.

So Ted got drafted and I got drafted and sent to South Korea. Ted went into combat, into the war, and I didn't. When he got out of the army and returned to Akiak he had post-traumatic stress disorder. He had survived the bullets, but he couldn't stand being back in Akiak. He had nightmares from all of the killings. He survived that, survived enemy bullets, but he couldn't survive alcohol. We actually ended up coming back to Akiak at almost exactly the same time, except that he came from Vietnam and I came from South Korea.

Frank taught me a lot when I was younger, but I was close with all of my brothers. Walter was one of the top sprint mushers in the Bethel region. He was the best in the west, you might say. In 1983 he competed in the Iditarod and finished in thirty-first place. That year Rick Mackey won and the race was still slower. It took longer than twelve days to take first place. Walter finished in over fifteen days.

For a while after that I kept asking him if he wanted to keep running the Iditarod and he said he did not. He said, "No, Mike, you do it. I'll just run the Kuskokwim 300." And that's what he did. He won all of the races around here for about ten years, the short ones and the middle-distance ones. For us, the Kusko 300 in Bethel, which everyone thinks of as the best and biggest middle-distance race, was even more important than the Iditarod.

Walter won all kinds of races in the area. All of our friends and family were there to watch him and he didn't have to travel to Anchorage to the starting line. He never captured the title in the Kusko 300, but he finished fourth twice. Walter really specialized in the village sprint races. He won the best sprint race in Bethel three years in a row. We went to Dillingham and he won that.

When we were kids we all pretty much did the same chores. Some of those chores involved taking care of the dogs. We trained the dogs at a young age. We took care of their feeding. We took care of their health. My dad usually had trained dogs to use for transportation by the time the pups grew up. We made leaders out of them. We did all the chores that needed to be done around the dog yard and we also helped with the hunting and fishing. Walter was a top racer and my brother Gerald—he was one of my favorite brothers—always helped me learn how to do things in the dog yard. He was my handyman fixing things when they broke.

Once, when we were small, Gerald threw an open can at me and it landed here on my eye. I still have a mark. I don't remember what he was mad about. I think it was a can of beef stew and the top cut me. It did some bleeding for a while. But Gerald was the one who helped me fish and we did a lot of fish tendering together for the local fish processor. We fished at the same time and that's how we made our money. He was always there for me.

Timmy Jr. was the youngest and he did the same thing as all of us. He did some work in the house and he helped raise the puppies. In a sense we were all trainers of the dogs. Fred, too. All six of the boys worked with the dogs and ran dogs.

When we were young my family attended the Moravian Church. My mom and dad and everybody in the village went to church on Sundays. It was our religion, but it was also a social occasion to bring everyone together. We didn't have TV and we didn't have extracurricular activities in town, so everybody went to church on Sundays. We did it consistently and we did it year-round. That helped make for a strong community, I think.

There was a strong belief in God. My parents wanted us to respect the God who controls all of the universe and all that he made. That is what they told us and what they taught us. Every week we had Sunday school teachers. Sunday was a very respected day in my family. My mom and dad did not want us to do anything on Sunday except to rest. That's what we did. It was a rest day. We didn't go out hunting or fishing. That was a big influence on me. The Elders were consistent with my mother and father. All the Elders who came to our house taught me about their belief in the Creator.

Those Elders, my parents, uncles, and people of those generations, grew up speaking Yupiaq. Some of them learned English, some of them did not. My generation, people now about sixty years old or more, was the first generation to focus on learning English. My generation made the shift. The older people were highly educated in Yup'ik ways and traditional teachings. Before contact with the whites they were very healthy people. They did not have problems with their teeth from eating sweets, diabetes, alcohol misuse, or any major regular health problems.

Our language and culture were intact. Our whole lives were complete then. But then contact came with gold miners, government workers, and missionaries starting in the late 1800s. They brought diseases that we had no immunity from, and they brought alcohol. It used to be that the Elders said if they heard about a death from a hundred miles away they cared about it and felt the same about that one death from far away as they did about one in their village. People had their own government, their own way of taking care of themselves, living off the land. They had a complete way of life that they enjoyed.

Obviously, things have changed. They changed with contact. The amount of deaths changed from smallpox, diphtheria, whooping cough, tuberculosis, and sexually transmitted diseases, too. Alcohol was brought in. People who had experienced their healthy way of life were subjected to trauma. At one time in Akiachak, which is only eleven miles from us, there was mass starvation because people couldn't take care of themselves. They had to dig mass graves and some of our relatives were among them.

That was as the result of first contact. It was a little bit what our brothers and sisters in Indian tribes in the Lower 48 experienced with the Trail of Tears—all of that loss of their land, death, war, alcohol, and the killing of women and children.

This was not something I was really conscious about when I was a kid, but the Elders would talk about it. They talked about what they had seen and the starvation and about the ways of living that were going away. They talked to us about that. In their youths they had the language, ways of life, culture, hunting, and fishing all set. They all had rules that were followed. Then first contact hit us right between the eyes. It is hard to imagine how much grief and trauma occurred. So many families could not take care of themselves. Then the missionaries came. The Moravians established an orphanage. Parents and other adults were wiped out. The Moravian orphanages were established because children could not take care of themselves. The Bureau of Indian Affairs started its schools. The goal was to provide education, but only up to the point of eighth grade and only in English. It was good to learn English, but they didn't have to ban the speaking of Native languages. Yupiaq was prohibited here.

If children spoke Yupiaq in school they were punished. Their mouths would be washed out with soap, or they would be hit for speaking their Native language. The teachers were instructed to assimilate the students with other American children. My mother told us stories about that. They were telling us that our way of life was not a good one and their way of life was better and we had to adapt.

Then Sheldon Jackson came around to establish missions and churches. He came to Alaska in 1877 and during his career it was said that he traveled more than a million miles and established more than one hundred missions and churches. Many of them were in Alaska and most of them were in the western part of the United States. He had it in his mind that he was going to save these lost Eskimo and Indian souls. His thinking was that these Yup'ik people are lost and our way of life is better. The feeling was that everyone had to learn English and that's that.

They taught English. It was made clear to us that it was important and useful to learn English, though in my mind it didn't have to be force-fed in such a harsh way. One missionary was a man named John Kilbuck, a Delaware Indian. He lived in Akiak and died here and he is the one who told people the importance of learning English. He said it was important to learn as much as we could about the ways of the white man because of what he had seen in the Lower 48. John Kilbuck had studied the history of Indians losing their lands, of being put on tribal reservations and before that the killing of women and children by the government. He was a witness to the Delaware Indians' loss of their land. He emphasized the story of the settlers and the farmers moving west and taking the land everywhere. He was trying to prepare us for the day that settlers were going to come to Alaska and take the land, to take the resources and put us in a box.

We consider the fish in the Kuskokwim River to be a resource. Fish has been a stable resource. We have had salmon forever, freshwater fish, whitefish, sheefish, burbot, pike, and blackfish. Fishing has been a resource for us. Moose, caribou, bear, and small game have been a very important staple of our diet, and we have been gathering berries and preserving them for winter forever. These have been ongoing practices from way back. I think my parents' generation was the first one to experience being punished for speaking the language, and attempts to change them to assimilate into the western way of life.

Alaska became a state in 1959, but the Indian Reorganization Act took effect in 1934. The federal government said that it had trust obligations in Alaska and to the Native tribes and tribal governments that were established. But there always seemed to be a lot of committees within governments somehow messing things up.

In my dad's generation there were changes. The introduction of alcohol and the opening of a liquor store in Bethel was a big thing. Bethel is less than thirty miles from Akiak by the river and even closer by air. The introduction and availability of alcohol began to affect things in Akiak.

By the time I came along, when I was young, people were drinking in Akiak. My parents drank alcohol. My grandparents got into alcohol. I would see a certain amount of violence because of alcohol in Akiak, though not as much as there was later. I grew up around alcohol. One of my grandmothers was not a drinker. She never drank. People drank, but the majority of people in Akiak did not drink yet. It was available, but not as many people abused it yet. That was just the beginning of easy availability of liquor in Bethel.

My father did some drinking, but then he thought about it. When one of my brothers died, and then a second brother died, my father decided to go cold turkey and not to drink again. Instead, he started a prevention program. There were changes that affected our lifestyle because of alcohol and now he wanted to prevent people from drinking alcohol and return to the way things were with a traditional lifestyle. I must have inherited that outlook from him, even if I didn't recognize it right away.

CHAPTER 5

I had picked out the Oregon College of Education to attend college and I was being awarded a small football scholarship, too, with plans to enroll in school in the fall of 1972. I was spending the summer fishing in Hydaburg in Southeast with some friends when the notice came to my home that I was being drafted into the United States Army.

In 1970, the government changed the draft to a lottery system based on your birthday. It was a random drawing that listed when you might be called to serve with numbers 1 through 365, for each day of the year. They did this for a few years and then dropped the lottery altogether. In 1972 I was one of the last draftees into the army.

I had to report in August. I had my physical done in Anchorage. I should have tried to get a deferment because of college, but I did not do that. I thought I would serve my time and then take advantage of the GI Bill to go to school. So I decided to follow through with the draft and report. They sent me to Fort Ord, California, for my basic training.

Fort Ord is near Monterey, California, a very pretty area. Up until that time, even though alcohol was becoming common in Akiak, I had never had a drink, never tasted beer. But at basic training we had weekends off to go to town sometimes and the guys would say, "Come with us. Come with us." That was the first time I tasted beer, my first Coors. I was twenty years old.

Although I had other plans for college in Oregon I wasn't opposed to going into the military. My dad was in the National Guard. I was familiar with the uniforms. He was in charge of the Akiak unit of the Alaska Army National Guard. He'd go to training periodically, so I had some idea about the military. And, of course, my oldest brother, Frank, was a veteran. He was in the National Guard by then and my second oldest brother, Ted, was in the army serving in Vietnam. I think the Williams family did its service to the US Army.

After I completed my basic training in California I had a couple of weeks off and I went to the Portland, Oregon, area for a visit. I had made friends with a bunch of guys from Native communities in that area and during the time I visited they had a bunch of basketball tournaments going on different reservations. I joined up with a team. I hooked up with a squad from Chemawa school and decided to play Indian ball for two weeks before resuming my army commitment. I was a five-foot-nine guard. That was how I spent my vacation from the army. Then I went back to California and it was somewhere between six and eight weeks later that I received orders that I was going to be deployed to South Korea. After I got the orders I got another two weeks off and went back to Portland to play some more basketball.

I was a private just starting out, but while I was at Fort Ord (which was closed in 1994) I was selected to be a platoon leader. That was a new form of leadership required and again part of my overall education. It was a very, very good experience. Between the leadership school and the army I was making a lot of friends from around the country. The interesting thing is that to go to South Korea I had to go back through Alaska. I flew from California to Seattle to Anchorage and then on to Seoul.

While we were fighting in Vietnam the army had a large presence in South Korea. And all of these years later there is still concern over the DMZ between South Korea and North Korea left over from the Korean War. That goes back to the time when I was born.

It was not a high alert operation at the time, though. It was peace time in Korea, though not in Vietnam. There was some tension at all times wondering about missiles being fired between the two Koreas. We were looking at the "Honest John" rocket missiles and we had ongoing training in case North Korea fired missiles. We were there for defensive purposes. There was always concern in the military about the whole peninsula area. At that time China loomed over things. There was always the feeling that China was North Korea's ally and that if something happened China with its huge population would get involved. I don't think that would occur today.

But really, nothing big happened like that while I was there. I was able to move around Korea quite easily. Actually, my appearance as an Alaska Native man was similar to the Koreans' so they would talk to me. I looked like them and I blended in very well with the Korean population. The language was different, of course, and their ways were a little different. But I took up tae kwon do, the martial arts discipline. Six days a week I trained at night after a day of work, practicing my karate-like skills. Two hours at a time six days a week. That's what I did with my evenings.

Taking up Asian martial arts was good for my body and my mind. It is not only a physical discipline. There is a mental toughness necessary. It did actually help me on the Iditarod Trail sometimes in terms of being able to withstand adversity. Sometimes during the Iditarod when things aren't going well and you are very tired and extremely cold and the dogs are having problems and not eating and you get dehydrated and sleep-deprived you go, *What the heck am I doing here?* You start to wonder if you should quit the race and go home. But that martial arts training, training consistently and training hard, made me a stronger person. I was able to defend myself—not to have a skill to beat up others—and had discipline. So I didn't quit.

I was in South Korea for six months. I also participated in traditional Korean festivities. I got interested in the culture, a new culture for me, and observed the special dates, the traditional dancing, and activities that Elders conducted. I liked the Korean language. It was different from what I had known, but I really enjoyed what they had to offer there.

In the army I got to know all kinds of people. Some were Native Americans, white guys, black guys. Some of them also took advantage of learning the Korean culture. But I also saw some things there that were negative that I had never seen before. There was some extreme segregation. There were bars specifically for black guys and specifically for white guys. There was also voluntary segregation in the army. If you went into the dining hall you would see white folks sitting over here and black folks sitting over there. They were just not mingling. It was strange to see that and it was the same way when soldiers went off the base, with white guys going here and black guys going there.

I was able to dance between the two races. I was able to be accepted by the white side and I was accepted on the dark side, the black side. I think about that time a lot. I also had a Polish friend and we talked about it a lot. I would say he was a real Polish guy and not a white guy. We would discuss this thing about whites and blacks not socializing. I said, "You're a Pole, not a white guy, even though your skin is white. I am an Alaska Native. I'm not a white guy or a black guy. Let's try something."

Since I was accepted by the black guys we decided to go over to a group of black guys and see what happened if we tried to mix. I told my friend, "You're a strong Polish person and let's try to convince them that you're not white, that you're a Pole." He agreed to see what would happen.

We walked into this black bar and we saw a table and took it. All of these black folks were looking at us and staring at my Polish friend. We just sat down and nobody said anything, but they were looking. After a little while I was served a beer, but they would not serve him. After another little while a couple of black guys came over and said, "Hey, what are you doing in our place? You don't see any white guys here. This is a black establishment."

At that point I said, "We talked about it before we came over here. This guy right here is not a white guy. He is a Pole and he doesn't consider himself to be a white guy. He's not a white guy. That's why we came over here." There were some back-and-forth exchanges and the black guys said, "Nah, you're a white guy." And my friend would say, "Nope, I'm a Pole. I'm not a white guy." Finally, after all of those exchanges—and we kept sitting there—he got a beer. At that bar we made lasting friends and we respected each other after that. We could return to that bar any time.

It didn't really surprise me that it worked out that way. I was not black. I was not white. I was accepted on both sides, so I could swing both ways. Why not him? It was pretty interesting. In the army was the first time I saw racial tension between guys who were supposed to be on the same side. They were on the same side, but segregated. I had followed the civil rights movement, but then here you had a guy, a good friend of mine, who was on the other side. His skin was white, and he didn't want to be considered a white guy, but a Pole.

I did start drinking in the army. I drank in the bars in South Korea, but not very much. After I finished my martial arts workout each night I went to a bar and had a couple of beers. I did not abuse alcohol at that time.

Being in South Korea for six months was a good experience all-around, but it was cut short. I suffered a detached retina in my right eye. I didn't know how it happened, whether it occurred during tae kwon do practice, or on the job with the military, but my eye was going blind. I couldn't see as well as I should have. I was losing vision and told the authorities I could only see a portion out of that eye. Within a week of me reporting it, since I couldn't really do anything for the army, I was mede-vaced from South Korea to San Francisco.

Then I was shipped to Fort Lewis in Tacoma, Washington. The plan was for me to have surgery in Seattle. Then they realized they didn't have the specialist they needed there and sent me back to San Francisco. They scheduled the eye surgery at Letterman General Hospital at the Presidio. When my eye was examined they diagnosed it as a detached retina and said that I was 40 percent blind in that eye.

They kept me around there after the operation and when I started to heal I played intramural basketball on the base. I was short, and there were all of these six-foot-seven hotshots around. But I played with them. I could jump. I was fast and I was a good shot.

What I wasn't doing much of was being a soldier while I was recovering. I really enjoyed my time in San Francisco. I wasn't doing them any good and after some time they decided to grant me a disability discharge. It wasn't as if my two years was nearly up as that they felt I could not perform at a top level. I received an honorable discharge with a disability.

That ended my army service. I had spent time in California, in Korea, Washington, and back in California. I had had some good experiences and seen some good cities, but in the winter of 1974 I was done and released from the army. I had seen a little bit of the world and I was ready to go back to Akiak.

CHAPTER 6

When I got out of the service I was around twenty-two years old and I missed home. Ted arrived back in Akiak a day before I did after combat in Vietnam. He started having nightmares about his time in the war.

Sometimes he kept his feelings inside and sometimes he talked about it. He mentioned how hard it was to adjust to Akiak after seeing all of that killing and what the army did to all of the villages and women and children there. It bothered him.

It was good for me to be back and hunting and fishing again. But there were no jobs in Akiak and I had the disability discharge from the army. I did have the GI Bill to use for school. After a few months in Akiak I decided to look for a job in Bethel. Bethel has more than 4,000 people so the odds were better I might find something. Also, Kuskokwim Community College is in Bethel, so I could take college courses.

I landed a job at the hospital doing kitchen duty and washing dishes. It paid pretty well and I enrolled at the college. I worked full-time and I took courses full-time. I got my own place and I was busy, busy, busy. I began studying behavioral health counseling. I wanted to be a mental health counselor.

This fit in with my plan of wanting to help others and I began studying for that degree. After washing dishes I got a job as the recreation director for the city of Bethel. I was nearly at black belt status in tae kwon do, so I wanted to do something using sports or physical education. I also was involved in karate. I began teaching an hour-and-a-half course each evening in karate at the recreation center. Then I was asked to teach karate at the high school, too, an extended hour. I was doing everything all at once for a while. I don't know how I fit everything into the day. I was taking sixteen hours, sixteen credits and doing all of that teaching, as well. I didn't have time to do anything except work, teach karate, and study.

It took me three years to complete that degree at the college. I spent a while washing dishes, but there was a psychiatrist in town named Verner Stillner and he took an interest in me. He was trying to get a mental health program started for kids through the Yukon-Kuskokwim Health Corporation.

He knew I was teaching karate to young people and he would see me in the kitchen. Sometimes he wanted to have lunch or dinner with me. I told him that I was studying to become a counselor and he was working at the mental health program in Bethel. He told me about the idea he had for the kids project. He wanted to help the Yup'ik people with their mental health issues and that there was a job opening on the outreach mental health staff for a counselor. Dr. Stillner was involved. Bridget Kline, a Yup'ik from Mountain Village, was involved. And so was a counselor by the name of Dana Kopunuk. He was an elderly guy that Dr. Stillner had recruited. He asked me to take the position. It was explained that I would have more educational opportunities to advance myself and that Mr. Kopunuk would be my mentor. So I took it. That fit in with my goals of being a basketball coach and helping young people. It's not the same as becoming a physical education teacher and a coach, but it is still helping.

It also offered more money than washing dishes. I had flexible time, too, not having to get up and start work in the kitchen at six o'clock in the morning.

The mental health program was the first in rural Alaska. It was an effort to come to grips with the issues that were affecting people. When I accepted the position I continued taking courses and Dr. Stillner ended up being one of my professors. I also took solo courses from him and he and his wife, Marianne (she was a psychiatric nurse who worked for the school district focusing on kids that had brain damage or developmental disabilities), joined my karate class and became my students.

When I took the mental health position it expanded my work with kids in the middle school. After a while Marianne Stillner asked me if I would be interested in using the karate instruction as a self-esteem and confidence builder for the kids that were brain damaged, had developmental disabilities, or didn't have any role models. We took some of those kids, equipped them with karate uniforms, and I spent two hours of my work day teaching them karate. I also worked as a counselor working through the schools in building self-esteem within these kids. These were kids who weren't doing well in the classroom and they had low self-esteem because of that or other reasons. After a year of doing that we found that these kids had improved their confidence and their grades. Everything improved for these kids.

This started in 1975 or 1976 and at the same time we had about thirty dogs in the kennel. My brothers were taking care of them, mainly Walter. But back then we always had around thirty dogs in our family for transportation and racing. It was pretty tough for me to spend too much time with the dogs because of all the things I was doing in Bethel during that period. But I took turns with getting fish for the dog food, feeding the dogs, and handling their sleds and equipment. I would go to Akiak on the weekends and mush the dogs. I kept my hand in with the dogs.

At about this time there was an explosion in suicide amongst young people in Alakanuk, which is a little bit more than 150 miles from Bethel. There seemed to be suicides happening every week. This was exactly the type of thing we were trying to prevent from happening in Bethel through our program. The Yukon-Kuskokwim Health Corporation was working with more than fifty tribes. We were trying to provide counseling services for the villages and it seemed as if Alakanuk was an important place to go.

It really did seem as if a teenager was killing himself, or herself, every week in Alakanuk. We wanted to help the community with its grieving. We wanted to find a way to be of assistance during this disaster. We wanted to examine the reasons why the kids were killing themselves.

What the heck was going on? The suicides prompted us to consistently travel to that village. I went there and met with community leaders, individuals who were affected, and families. We were trying to salve the wounds. We really wanted to stop this epidemic of suicides and address the issue of "How do we prevent more wounds?" We went there trying to look for underlying causes.

It seemed pretty clear to us that some of the underlying causes of this despair involved the loss of their language and the loss of the culture. And alcohol was playing a major part. Some kids were being abused. There was dysfunction in families as the result of dependency on alcohol. People were drinking because they weren't adjusting to quick life changes from the days of the healthy Alaska Native. There was that pressure to assimilate. There were all of those new government rules. There was rapid change stemming from the Alaska Native Claims Settlement Act. Some people got rich. Some people were still on the outside. Families that for generations had been solidly relying on subsistence hunting and fishing were going on welfare, public assistance.

All of these things add up to loss of identity and lack of identity—loss and lack. Those were the underlying issues and they still are outstanding issues in villages in rural Alaska. We still have to figure out what to do about those underlying causes. All of those things, language, land, religion, education, alcohol dependency, education, contribute to the loss of identity. It is not difficult to feel overwhelmed.

We felt it was very important to identify people at risk as early as possible and put them in a controlled environment before they attempted suicide. We could remove them from their everyday life. A controlled environment is the Alaska Psychiatric Institute or the Crisis Intervention Service in Bethel, somewhere they can be watched for seventy-two hours. Once you are admitted that is the rule, to stay for seventy-two hours.

I looked at my job as someone who was trying to be part of the solution, to help to fix the underlying problems. Only at the time things were getting worse. Suicides were going on in several villages and then people started killing each other. The violence was growing. People in rural Alaska were killing themselves and killing each other and most of the time alcohol was involved.

We succeeded at helping in Alakanuk to some degree. One thing that happened was that we started "talking circles" as a way to help people open up with their feelings and talk about what was bothering them. To this day there are talking circles out there in villages for this purpose. If there is any suspicion that a person might want to harm himself the others talk to him and try to get him removed from his life and put under observation to stop it.

But people were also killing other people. I was working hard, going to school, studying, and traveling to villages. After three years of that pace I got burned out. I said that I could only handle so many suicides and so many homicides in my life and at that time I also met Maggie, the woman who would become my wife. That was around 1976. She was in Akiachak and worked as an accountant and bookkeeper for several villages. When I first met her she was managing their money.

I was also still trying to play basketball whenever I could and I was on the Akiak team when it traveled to other villages for tournaments. I would get eighty or more points every tournament. I averaged a lot of points. I was good. My shot was excellent. The scouting report on me was that if a defense was going to try to stop me they had to shut down my jump shot. But they didn't. They never could stop me. We won so many tournaments. In Akiachak, Maggie would come to watch the games.

Maggie was a basketball fan and I noticed her when she came to watch. She was a young, small, pretty little girl whom I wanted to meet. The way I remember it, no one really introduced me, but I took the initiative. I think I introduced myself. There was a big rivalry between Akiak and Akiachak, but we won most of the games at the time and I scored most of the points.

I think my points impressed the girls. I think I made a big impression on Maggie. Maggie liked my game. She was from Akiachak, but got a job working in Bethel. So we were both in Bethel. Then she decided to take additional training at Alaska Business College in Anchorage for a while. Then she returned, but she spent weekends in Akiachak. I bought her Christmas presents and on the weekends I would visit her.

Maggie lived in the Bethel apartments with running water and amenities. I lived in a housing project. One winter day the power plant burned down in Bethel and I didn't have any heat. My water froze, too. But Maggie had emergency electricity and running water. She ended up feeding me at her apartment and allowed me to stay and take showers there. I think the power plant burning down solidified us getting together and we eventually got married and we have been married for more than thirty-eight years.

We have had six children. The oldest is Ted, who is thirty-seven. Ted works on construction and fixing houses. Sheila, who became the executive director of our tribe, is next. She works for Akiak Native Community and runs all of the programs in Akiak. Shawna is nearing her college degree. Mike Jr. is the current Iditarod musher in the family and he works at construction, too, when he is not training dogs. He is building his house for his family. There was Timothy, the youngest boy, and Thea.

The fifth one was Timatheen. When she was nine years old Maggie and I and one of our cousins were riding a four-wheeler with Timatheen. She was sitting in the front and got distracted by some kids playing on the side of the road. She fell off and hit her head on the gravel. We were only traveling about one mile per hour, but she fell forward, fell on her head, and suffered a hematoma and she died from it.

It was a terrible accident. That was the most painful experience that I ever had. It was just like a knife going through the heart. It was so painful watching her die like that. Maggie held her in her arms for hours, until they took her to Anchorage by medevac. She passed away in Anchorage. We were there and we had to pull the plug. It was so sad. After Timatheen passed away, a baby was born to a cousin of mine who was fifteen years old when she got pregnant. She was too young to be a mother and her family asked us if we would like to adopt a little girl, and we said yes. So we adopted Christine, who is now fifteen. When we adopted Christine it helped us a lot with the healing process.

Maggie had been working as a teacher's aide in the school system, but after the accident she decided she wanted to go back to school full-time to obtain her teaching degree. I encouraged her to go to summer school. After we lost Timatheen we spent summers in Fairbanks for four years while Maggie attended the University of Alaska Fairbanks summer school. Part of it was teleconference classes on the computer, too.

We sacrificed our summers of subsistence fishing. We would go away every summer. Maggie got her degree, passed her teacher's tests, and became a certified teacher. Doing it in four years was pretty commendable, I thought, and after what we went through with Timatheen, too.

CHAPTER 7

After I got burned out on the counseling from seeing too much death and too many wasted lives I decided to take a break. I came back to Akiak and in 1977 took a job as business manager of the local corporation. Maggie was pregnant with Ted and I obtained materials and planned to build my own house.

The house was twenty-four feet by thirty-two feet and we felt it would be big enough for me and Maggie and our coming child. I thought it was a pretty big house when I first moved in and it was going to be a temporary house. But even after we kept having kids we never moved. I have lived in the same house for thirty-seven years.

When I was in high school in Oregon I learned carpentry skills. I learned how to build at the Chemawa Indian School. My brothers helped me and I hired a few other people to help. But I did most of it. I did part of everything and I really enjoyed putting this together. The only thing we did was enlarge the back porch as the number of kids increased. We couldn't fit them all on it.

We have been in the same house so long that my kids who grew up there are grown, have their own spouses and have their own children. I am the grandfather of eight, Orian, Tsion, Kailee, Ava, Megan, Thea, Kohle, and Daniel. I have one great-grandchild, Sarah, our latest addition.

Tsion is pronounced Zion. I think Ted got that out of the Bible. It's a Jewish name. My oldest son, Ted, thinks he is a Jewish person. He supports the Jewish people. He's got an Israeli flag at his house and Jewish symbols. I told him, "You're not Yup'ik, you're Jewish."

At the time I came back to Akiak the village corporation was close to bankruptcy. We had consultants and people didn't know how to handle money. I became the business manager and I did it for two years. I needed time off from counseling and wanted to do something else. The corporation needed someone and I decided to manage the business. It was a different work environment from mental health counseling. It was easy for me to focus on trying to solve the problems of a corporation on the verge of bankruptcy. The local people had had trouble managing the business end. There was no one with experience. For all of us it was hard going from being a hunter-gatherer-fisherman to overnight becoming a business manager.

When I returned to Akiak I also returned to more traditional living. I hunted and fished more often again. I had really missed that and I came back to the subsistence lifestyle. Upon my return I was elected to the tribal council for the Akiak Native Community. It's a federally recognized tribe. Maggie had a job at the school.

After I became business manager we started selling lumber. We started selling gas and oil. We started selling goods and started the local store. We paid off all of our bills and then we generated more money, increased the profits, and stabilized the corporation. I oversaw that and it was very difficult. We had to make good investments, where we put our money. We put money into interest-bearing accounts. I had fun doing that, making money for the corporation. I believed that tribes could start businesses. Why have a Native corporation if you didn't?

This all stemmed from the Alaska Native Claims Settlement Act. President Richard Nixon signed it into law on December 18, 1971. I was still in high school. I even took a class on the Alaska Native Claims Settlement Act. We learned about the federal government's responsibilities, the land trade, the start-up of Alaska Native corporations, and the politics. Under federal law the government has a responsibility to protect the tribes. It is under the jurisdiction of the secretary of the interior. Lands were put in trust status. They are reserved lands that are the property of the sovereign tribes and cannot be sold. They cannot be tapped. This brings us back to the government in Washington, D.C. making those treaties with the Indians in the Lower 48 and breaking every one of them. We had to be educated about the Alaska Native Claims Settlement Act and learn our rights.

Former Alaska governor Walter Hickel had been appointed secretary of the interior in the Nixon administration and he acted as a negotiator between the Alaska Federation of Natives and the state of Alaska. The act transferred Alaska lands to twelve newly created Native corporations. Later, a thirteenth corporation was created representing Alaska Natives who live outside of the state. The settlement provided Alaska Natives with 44 million acres of land and $963 million.

It is the responsibility of the United States government to protect the tribes. Of course the United States government has not lived up to its obligations. In some places tribes have gone to court to win the rights they had. It is no wonder that no American Indian or Alaska Native trusts the US government. The government owes us big-time.

When I was in school and took the course about the Alaska Native Claims Settlement Act the conclusion of the class was that this was the biggest rip-off in the history of Alaska. We thought it was a bad settlement. It took away our hunting and fishing rights. It extinguished our original title to lands and disenfranchised children that were born after December 18, 1971. In essence it said that there would not be any more Indian country here. Natives would be under state jurisdiction. The state would have control over Native land. That was unheard of with Indian tribes, except in Menominee, Wisconsin. They had a similar land settlement that put the tribe into a Native corporation. The Menominees' woes started then. They started losing land. The land was in a vulnerable position for sales.

The federal government terminated the tribe in the 1950s, making it subject to state law. The Menominee tribe went to court to ensure its hunting and fishing rights. The case went to the Supreme Court and in

1968 the tribe won with a ruling that said it did not surrender its hunting and fishing rights. In 1973 the tribe again won federal recognition in Congress and in 1975 the reservation was reestablished.

The land where my house is located is a restricted deeded lot and it is deeded to me. This is sovereign ground protected by the US Department of the Interior. This is not simple land. It is trust land. But just a hundred yards from here, the Native Corporation lands are fee simple. The Native Corporation owns the land, but is under the jurisdiction of the state of Alaska for management.

Alaska manages the mammals. The state manages the fish and game. That is because we are under the jurisdiction of the state. The Native corporations are state-chartered, for-profit corporations and they're owned by the shareholders of each village corporation and the shareholders of the regional corporations. The title underneath the land belongs under state rules. Our tribe right now, the Akiak Native Community, has no land. The corporation does. That is separate and distinct from the tribe.

Native corporations are not governments. They are businesses. They are just businesses that the for-profit corporations use to make money under charter for their shareholders. I'm a shareholder. I spent those years as business manager and I worked with state rules and federal rules and could play by those rules to make money for Akiak. Anybody could do that. I could have done that forever and made a lot of money. I could have gotten rich and had the highest salary in Akiak and lived a good life for me.

But what about the children? The children who were born after 1971 have no shares. None of my children or grandchildren own shares, not even the oldest children. They have no shares in the village corporation. They have nothing. They have no land. They are tribal members, but the tribe doesn't have land. It's under the management of the Native corporation.

It was fun to make money for the corporation and I could have done that forever, but I am also on the tribal council. I know the word *sovereignty* and I know what tribal sovereignty means. It means we have inherent sovereignty over our individual lives. We have a sovereign right to regulate and make laws in our village and manage our village the way we see fit, the way we have been doing it for thousands of years. Sovereignty also means we could start businesses. We could do anything we want to protect our lands and our territories. But that sovereignty has eroded because of the passage of the Alaska Native Claims Settlement Act.

Who in their right mind would agree to extinguish our hunting and fishing rights? We never agreed to that. Those framers, those people, they never agreed to eliminate our hunting and fishing rights. They said, "We'll deal with that later. If there's a problem we'll restore things later." Later was the Alaska National Interest Lands Conservation Act of 1980. That was supposed to restore our hunting and fishing rights. But instead they changed what was supposed to be Native preference to rural preference. They slashed that Native preference and made the change because of non-Natives living in rural areas. In some places, like Akiak, for practical purposes, that is almost the same. Akiak is probably 99 percent Native. But that doesn't mean that is right and it is not the same everywhere.

We always had hunting and fishing rights as Alaska Natives. That's what we do. That's what we live for. We have to live. We have to eat. We have to do that and that's what we have been doing for thousands of years before anybody else showed up. And we need to have that customary and traditional right to practice hunting and fishing as we have for thousands of years. However, then commercial and sportfishing came in. That should have nothing to do with us, but it does. We never agreed to the Alaska Native Claims Settlement Act. We never voted for it. We didn't agree to extinguish our hunting and fishing rights. We didn't agree to extinguish our original title to the land.

The Supreme Court said that the lands are under state jurisdiction and the Native corporations are not sovereign governments and if all of the land is under state jurisdiction it cannot be classified as Indian country.

A construction company from Unalakleet was building a school in Venetie and Venetie said, "Let's tax this construction company 5 percent above the land money so we have money to run our government. The tribe said, "We're taxing you for building this school because it's a business." The state contested that and said the tribe had no authority to tax a business because the land was allocated to them on a fee simple basis.

After three years of working as business manager in Akiak I decided that was enough. I really missed counseling and about 1980 I got back into it in Akiak and a lot of the work involved substance abuse. I had been working with suicide cases and other mental health issues, schizophrenics, and people with developmental disabilities. But there was an opening for a substance abuse counselor for the village of Akiachak. That is only eleven miles from Akiak.

By then the issue of alcohol abuse was hitting home within my own family, too.

CHAPTER 8

At about this time, around 1980, my own family began having terrible trouble with alcohol. I was seeing the worst of the problems up close in the worst way. My brothers were drinking heavily and my brother Ted was the first death we had because of alcohol.

He was the one who came out of the army and got to Akiak within a day of me. He had been back only three months. He was tormented and he overdosed on alcohol. He was drinking at a friend's house down the street and he just passed out and died. Right after he returned he just kept drinking and drinking. That was really when my dad decided to stop drinking. Ted was not very old, about twenty-five, when he passed away.

My first reaction when I heard Ted had died was, "Oh, damn. I don't believe it."

I couldn't believe that he was gone.

He was a young man and so was Frank. He was twenty-nine or thirty. Frank was in Bethel on a snowmachine and after drinking he went out on the Kuskokwim River and the snowmachine went into open water. His body was never found. He drank too much before he left or on the way home and went through the ice. He had been traveling with a friend and his friend made it home, but Frankie did not.

Frank's death hurt me very much. My thoughts were so bad about it. What a way to go, to waste your life, to waste his life. He had so much skill and was so knowledgeable about hunting and fishing and survival in the wilderness, and then to have too much to drink and drive a snow-machine in the winter after drinking. What a big, big waste.

I was home in Akiak and somebody said that Frankie had gone through the ice into the water and we ran to check it out. There was a search and the first thing that was found was a bottle floating on top of the open water in a hole in the ice. It was a plastic bottle of whiskey and it was almost empty. Then we found the snowmachine. It was so hard to receive the word when something like that happens.

My reaction was the same as with Ted. I found it hard to believe they were gone. Even with all of that happening the Williams brothers continued to consume alcohol. I can't explain that. I was really close with my brothers, especially Frank. That was really my first and strongest reaction, disbelief.

Then my brothers Walter and Timmy came up from Bethel in 1989 with some friends and they were partying. After that they got into a boat in rough waters on the river. Timmy was driving the boat and it snapped in half. He drowned. Walter was there, but he and a friend survived that. It was another terrible accident. We couldn't find Timmy's body at first. Maybe two months later he was found when the body came to the surface downriver. Somebody found him alongside the water, stuck on a piece of a tree. His body stunk so badly and he had puffed up and was unrecognizable, so it was a closed-casket funeral. That was my third brother to die in an alcohol-related incident. Alcohol had a very strong hold on us.

My brother Gerald was the fourth one who passed away. Gerald and a friend were on the Kwethluk River. They had ordered some booze from someplace that they picked up and they were drinking in Bethel. The boat hit a piece of wood and Gerald flew off the boat into the water and drowned. The guy driving the boat lived and he got the word out after he was pulled out of the water. But Gerald could not be found at first either. A couple of weeks later, about two weeks probably, his body was recovered. That was in June of 1993. At the time I had been attending a Rural Providers Conference in Nenana and was just about to travel home when I heard about Gerald. My thinking was I wasn't the only one at that conference going home to attend funerals. These were drownings, overdoses, and accidents and they were all alcohol-related.

In the case of Gerald, who was thirty-six, he was making progress on sobriety. It was hard for me to accept. One brother after another lost to alcohol. That left just me, Walter, and Bucko. I just could not believe that these Alaska Natives kept drinking and then getting into their boats and driving them on the rivers and they did not even carry life preservers. The same type of thing happened again and again.

Walter was splitting his time between Akiak and Bethel. My mother was working in Bethel at the time. Walter traveled back and forth between the two places, working and spending time with his family. One day when he stayed in Bethel Walter was boiling hot water. He was drinking alcohol at the same time, I think. While he was making the hot water he turned on the electric stove. Then he passed out cold. The kettle kept going with the water and Walter was unconscious. After the water boiled, eventually it evaporated, but the kettle was still on the burner. Over time while Walter was passed out the heat melted the aluminum kettle. A fire started and the fumes from the fire and smoke inhalation killed him. Walter didn't make it. He suffocated.

We called my brother Fred "Bucko." He was at my mother's house and he made up some home brew alcohol. For some reason after drinking that stuff he must have been depressed. He went and got a shotgun and shot himself to death. That was my sixth brother who died because of alcohol over a period of about eight years. Six brothers I lost and all in a short time.

Our grieving was so strong. My mother had a very difficult time, especially with Timothy. That was something. So I know a little about grief and disaster from personal experience. My family went through its own disaster. I was a counselor. I am a helper. I was trying to help my brothers and trying to help my family and while doing all of that, coping with all of that, I almost went crazy. Facing all of those deaths was the hardest thing in my life. The grieving and healing process was so hard. It seemed to never end.

One of the things that kept me going after all of my brothers were gone were the dogs. We still had the kennel. Now it was up to me to keep it going. Working with the sled dogs was my therapy. The dogs helped me deal with all of those issues. I ran out of brothers and I was the last one standing. I was nearly overwhelmed by the emotions of what had happened. I was definitely feeling sorry for myself and was depressed.

The dogs helped pull me out of that depression. I got to thinking that after so many negative things I wanted to do something positive. I wanted to do something in memory of my brothers and not just let them rest in their graves. I knew it would be easy to keep feeling sorry for myself, and it would be easy to do nothing. I told myself I needed to fight back and do something positive, so that they would not be forgotten lying in their graves. Somehow I wanted to get the word out about them. I did not want anyone else to have to go through what I did and my family did. My mother, my wife, Maggie, my children, all went through this, losing a brother-in-law, uncles. We also had a counselor to help us. Elizabeth Sonny Boy used to come to the house and help us with the healing process. She did a lot of good work for us. But there are different kinds of healing. My family and I were healed in the sense that we don't think about the ruined lives of my brothers every day and what they could have done. But I am very angry that it happened. I am bitter that it happened. I am still very bitter, very angry. Years have passed. I am angry at alcohol. Alcohol is the enemy. All of those lives were cut short and my brothers would have had children, so many members of the Williams family never came to be because those brothers died at an early age and did not become family men or have children later.

It was in my mind that I would fight alcohol for the rest of my life. Alcohol stared me in the face every day and I said I would have to fight it every day. I became a representative on the Kuskokwim Health Corporation. I spent a lot of time asking why this happened to my brothers. Six of them dead—that is like a total of war casualties from a battle. I began to think of life as a war, a war against alcohol. It is a battle. It seems impossible for one family to be affected and afflicted like that, but it happened to my family.

And yes, there were times when I thought, *Why not me?* I was the only one left of the men in my generation, the seventh brother. I think that I was spared by the Creator. I don't really know. I feel like I was spared to do something of value. I must have been born to do something. The Creator seemed to give me strength. I really have had faith in God to protect me and my family. But my brothers were in my family and they had virtually the same loving and caring upbringing. Yet they succumbed to alcohol.

I could also have followed my brothers to an early grave because of alcohol. I first drank when I was in the army and I did get drunk. I drank whiskey and beer. I got drunk, but I did not drink dangerously. It was getting drunk with the guys for fun, but I did not drink so seriously I could not take care of myself. When I got out of the army I continued to drink. I drank when I got home from South Korea in the 1970s and I drank until almost the end of the 1980s. Most of it was just social drinking. Sometimes, though, I did get drunk badly and had way too much to drink.

It is very possible that because of my role in the Sobriety Movement or by carrying signatures in the dogsled during the Iditarod that many Alaskans believe that Mike Williams has never had a drink in his life. That is not true. I got caught up in drinking to excess. I would call myself a recovering alcoholic. I'm not in denial. Given what I have seen in my lifetime I would say I am an alcoholic and when you're recovering, you're recovering forever. So I am still recovering even though I am sober.

This is me saying that I am alcoholic. This was self-diagnosis. I would say I reached that conclusion in 1988. In the beginning I never thought that way. I was a social drinker and I didn't think I had a problem. I would drink sometimes when I went out with people, starting with my fellow soldiers in the army, but I also drank when I got home. I never even thought about having a problem with alcohol. But in the end it was a problem. I was just thinking I would go out with the guys and have a few drinks. I'll just have a few. No big deal, but that didn't make me a problem drinker.

I was even drinking when I was a counselor on substance abuse. I just didn't see abuse in me. Again, not a problem for me. My brothers drank so much that they died because of it and I still didn't see it as a problem for me. I was just thinking I was drinking for fun. Those other people had big problems. I started drinking more after my brothers died in those alcohol-related incidents. I was trying to numb myself. I know it does not make much sense. It is ironic that I was trying to feel better through using alcohol, the substance that killed them. I was trying not to feel grief about my brothers' deaths. I chose to do it with alcohol, not in a healthy way. Here I was a counselor and I was not counseling myself. I was doing exactly the wrong thing when I should have known better. But it was all driving me crazy and it was hard to cope with losing all of my brothers.

Then Maggie stepped up to me and said that I had to stop drinking. I absolutely had to stop. She said, "It's either me and the family, or the bottle. If you are not wise enough, if you do not wise up and deal with this issue, I'm gone." Maggie talked to me and said, "Enough is enough." That made the decision for me. I decided, "Yep, I'm going to stop drinking." So I did. I went cold turkey. It was a huge struggle in the beginning. It was very tough for the first three months.

When Maggie confronted me about my drinking that was a big shock. It was like getting hit over the head by a hammer. She was very serious about it. Right away I thought, *Geez, I'm going to lose my wife. I'm going to lose my children. What am I gonna do?* It was a powerful message. I chose Maggie.

What I did was stay away from my friends who drank. I stayed away from almost everybody. These people were what you would call bad influences when it came to drinking, so I stopped hanging out with them. I spent more time with the dogs than people. The dogs were good therapy. I had to take care of them. I could take rides out into the backcountry and spend time alone in the wild. The dogs were very good for me.

A lot of people might say that is an easy choice to make, to choose your wife and family over drinking, but it's not an easy thing to stop if you feel you are addicted. That's hard. There were some very hard moments in there. It was a huge challenge. I think when I started the real healing over losing my brothers and discontinued drinking to mask my emotions that I did a better job of dealing with my grief. Elizabeth Sonny Boy helped. Several Elders spoke to me and they were helpful talking to me. They were not just standing by and watching. They came and talked to me and offered a lot of support. It was a nightmare with all of those deaths. There is only so much grief a person can stand.

I don't know if I ever really got angry at my brothers who kept drinking after the first couple of them died. But they were stupid to keep drinking and taking chances. They made mistakes. It should have been obvious that we all had to stop drinking after Ted and Frankie died. But we didn't. Later, I just thought of it as stupidity.

The other thing I thought a lot about, besides Maggie's ultimatum, was that I might die from an alcohol incident, too. I was going around feeling threatened by it. I thought, *I'm gonna be next.* All of my brothers were gone and I thought I might be joining them. I thought, *I'm gonna be gone like the rest of them if I don't stop.*

I had a lot of reasons to live. I had a wife, children, a job, a house, a big family, a lot of people that loved me. That was all pretty good motivation to keep going and to stop drinking. I kept taking care of the dogs and I kept racing. I was in my midthirties when I stopped drinking, so I have to think I stopped at the right time.

The dogs became a substitute, too. I put more and more time into them, taking care of them, feeding them, training them, racing them. I thought a lot about my brothers being gone and how I had a lot of responsibility to my family and to help their families, but the dogs also filled a need. I threw myself into long-distance mushing. Between 1988 and 1991 I spent a lot of time with the dogs and changing my life. I told myself I was going to put the old life behind me and start over from that age.

It has been more than twenty-five years since I last had a drink. I am sober, but I do not fool myself. I know that I am still a recovering alcoholic. I thank God that I was able to begin recovery and that I did not end up dead like all of my brothers.

*Above: Hunting camp
1985.*

*Left: Working with dogs
and fishing for food have
always been a part of
Mike Williams's life.
This picture was taken
in 1978.*

Left: A younger Mike Williams when he was first doing the Iditarod about twenty years ago.

Below: The dog lot in Nome after finishing the Iditarod.

The starting line in Anchorage.

Mushing on the ice.

At fish camp. This is Mike's wife, Maggie.

The life-giving Kuskokwim River can be a handful when it floods.

*Left: Mike's reputation as
a musher battling sobriety
issues has gained support
in many ways.*

*Below: Coming into the
finish in Nome.*

Above: Mike is a popular guy along the Iditarod Trail and is given warm welcomes at the checkpoints.

Left: Wrapped up in warm clothes and ready to go at the Iditarod start in Anchorage.

CHAPTER 9

Dog mushing really became a much bigger part of my life. These days I have an older poster on the inside of the front door that reads, "Mike Williams Never Races Alone." That refers to my deceased brothers, who are with me in spirit in my mind. The poster has a picture of me on the back of my sled in the background. But it also has photographs of my brothers who are gone, Ted, Frankie, Bucko, Gerald, Timmy, and Walter.

It also says, "The Iditarod is the longest, hardest, and greatest dogsled race of them all. As in many other human efforts, it takes a team to win and the Iditarod is no exception. Mike, a Yup'ik Eskimo from Akiak, Alaska, has been on the trail for nine races now and for a lot of those races American Seafoods and Coastal Villages Region Fund have been there with him as his major sponsors, part of the team that keeps the dogs fed and the bills paid.

"But before the sponsors provided the money, Mike's brothers provided the dream and the inspiration. Because all six of Mike's brothers died of alcohol-related accidents, Mike mushes in their memory and for the cause of sobriety. So when the cold wind blows on the long and lonely trail, Mike is never alone. His brothers are softly calling from the shadows, from the clouds, from the mist, and from the night. Mush on Mike, mush for all of us. Never quit. Never tire. Never stop. Live your dreams for us so that we may live in you. Mike may not come in first every time, but as Mike says, 'When you do what you love for those that you love, you're always a winner.'"

I mush to honor the memory of my brothers. Just the other day a reverend who was visiting Akiak came knocking on my door. Someone had told him to look me up, for religious reasons, for a program he was involved in. But when he saw the poster on the door, he went, "Oh, you're Mike Williams. You're that Mike Williams." He knew my name from the Iditarod.

My brother Walter was a very good musher. He was one of the best. He won a lot of races in the villages and he came close to winning the Kuskokwim 300. Walter and I were the ones who spent the most time training my dad's dogs, first as pups, though that was after we joined Frankie in the training. But when I went to high school in Oregon, into the army, and worked in Bethel, in my absence, Walter did most of it. He continued to work with the dogs and he raced them.

One of the other top mushers always around at that time was John Phillip. One year he raced in the Anchorage Fur Rendezvous world championship with only five dogs and he came in fifth place. And all of those other top racers, Roland Lombard, and more, wanted to buy those five dogs. Some teams have twenty dogs in them at the Rondy. But John would never let those dogs go. His grandson, Gilbert Phillip, married one of my daughters and is my son-in-law.

When John traveled from Akiak to the Anchorage area he stayed with Joe and Vi Redington in Knik or Stan Barney. John and my dad had these red dogs. We sold a red dog to Susan Butcher, who won four Iditarods, and we sold one to Rick Swenson, who won five Iditarods. Those red dogs came out of Brownie, a dog that Myron Angstman had for years in Bethel. Rick and Susan split those litters and one of those big red dogs became Susan's leader when she was working her way up in the Iditarod. That was before she had Granite, her great leader. Now John Baker from Kotzebue, who won the Iditarod in 2011, has a black leader from the breed that came out of Akiak.

Walter and I kept mushing and raising dogs and when I was living outside of Akiak he trained the dogs with my oldest brother, Frankie. Walter did most of the racing. I helped him in different ways when he went to the villages to compete. I helped get the food and equipment ready. He raced in Akiak, in villages, in Bethel, and in Elia Sallafie and won three in a row. He got that trophy three times. He teamed up with his friend James Nicholai and mushed the dogs to Aniak. Walter and James took eighteen dogs to Aniak to race once, I think. That was before the Kusko started.

The Kuskokwim 300 started in Bethel in 1980 and it began offering the biggest purse money of any middle-distance race and really of any race besides the Iditarod. It was one of the biggest events of the year around here. Myron Angstman did a lot to promote it and build it. Even in the first race the field was tremendous and many top mushers came. Rick Swenson won the first Kusko. Susan Butcher came in second and Joe Redington came in third.

When I moved back to Akiak from Bethel, Walter and I worked together again in the kennel doing what we always did. In that sense it was as if I had never been away. Walter did the 1983 Iditarod. Up until he passed away Walter did most of the racing.

We were always going to Anchorage for the Fur Rendezvous. The Fur Rendezvous is a sprint race. It is a stage race where the dogs run either twenty or twenty-five miles each day for three days. It is not a long-distance race and it is not like the Iditarod where you keep going as far as you can for as long as you can between sleeping and eating. In those days Iditarod dogs were much bigger. Some might be malamutes. The sprint dogs were leaner and smaller. When we were at the Fur Rondy the other mushers were saying things like, "Hey, these look like Iditarod dogs. They're tough. They're big. They seem to have good feet and they have good fur and I bet they eat well." So the others mushers planted the idea that we should do the Iditarod and Walter tried it once.

Mostly, though, Walter and I did the sprint scene and got to know everyone like George Attla, Roxy Wright, Gareth Wright, and even Emmitt Peters. We sold some dogs to Roxy. We must have come to Anchorage for the Rondy for fifteen years. We made some great friends, people like Charlie Champaine and Joee Redington. Joee raced the Rondy instead of becoming a long-distance musher like his father, Joe.

Dick Tozier, who was the Rondy race marshal, and later had the Tudor Track renamed for him, was the one who really helped us and encouraged us. It is expensive to travel from Akiak to Anchorage and even more so if you are transporting a dog team. It is very difficult for rural Alaskans who live off the road system to make the journey without drawing down their bank accounts a lot. Dick would find us a place to stay and dog trucks for us to use while we were in Anchorage. Because Walter was winning all of those races in the villages, in Dillingham, up the Yukon in St. Mary's, we really wanted to be part of the Fur Rendezvous.

Although the Rondy has changed in recent years, in the early 1980s it was a still a big party. People came from everywhere to the winter carnival. The races were on the radio first and then they were televised. Rondy was the biggest deal in town. Before the villages had TV people used to gather around the radio in the kitchen or living room and listen to the Rendezvous. They had helicopters in the air tracking the race and following the mushers. It was the best. Dick Tozier was the best, too, given how much he helped us. I got to know other people who were characters in Rondy sprint mushing like Orville Lake and Earl and Natalie Norris.

That was our background in mushing, in races that were over in about an hour or so. We weren't racing any distances and we weren't out there overnight camping. The race went off during the day, we ran the race, packed up the dogs, and either went home or went to the place we were staying because the race would continue for another day. When we entered the Iditarod in 1983 we didn't know what we were doing. When Walter went out on the trail we didn't send out any human food. We didn't send out any extra equipment for the trail. We didn't send out extra batteries for a headlamp. Mostly we sent out fish for the dogs to eat. We didn't have processed, high-nutrient food for the dogs. We also didn't have a lot of money, so it was a shoestring race for us.

We put everything we had in the sled and off he went. I didn't know what Walter was going to do for food in the wilderness. He said he always drank juice in the checkpoints and he ate frozen fish, dried fish.

The Iditarod is a thousand miles long and at that time the pace of the race was slower, so you knew you were going to be out there for a while and could easily face life-threatening weather. Rick Swenson did a nice thing. He saw what Walter was eating and drinking and talked to him. Then Swenson got the word out that Walter had a minimum amount of food on trail. Under the rules it is legal for mushers to help one another. So Rick made sure that at each checkpoint Walter had a care package for him and the dogs so he had enough food. Everyone helped him out.

I made sure to be in Nome at the finish line when Walter came in, but it wasn't easy. I was in Anchorage and right after the Iditarod started my uncle died. I returned to Akiak and buried him and then I returned to Anchorage. Since so many people were going to the finish in Nome, I hitchhiked from Anchorage on planes and stopped in some checkpoints. But I beat Walter to Nome and was standing there in the morning when he came in with a time of 15 days, 23 hours, 17 minutes.

Along the way to Nome Walter got some beaver meat from a trapper to feed to the dogs. But he sliced his hand open with a knife while cutting the beaver meat. The veterinarians sewed him up and gave him a shot of Novocain. He could have scratched with a bad hand, but he kept going and finished. He spent a lot of time mushing with Vern Halter and Shannon Poole. After he finished Walter made a point to thank Rick Swenson for the assistance and said the trip was pretty enjoyable. A lot of times when mushers cross the finish line in Nome—especially if they were beat up by the weather or in crashes, they immediately say that they will never do the Iditarod again. Some people get so enthusiastic about the race that they don't even want it to end and they promptly say they will be back the next year.

Walter did not say either one of those things. The thing that I remember him saying was, "Well, I'm glad I made it. I made the trip." That was what he said about doing the Iditarod, but he didn't say he wanted to race again and he didn't say he never planned to race again. Pretty soon, though, when I asked Walter if he wanted to do the Iditarod anymore, he said he did not. He said, "No, I'll do the village races and the Kusko, but if you want to do the Iditarod, you do it because I am not."

Some years before Walter raced someone did a study on Iditarod mushers, sort of profiling. And there have been other university studies from different places over the years trying to sum up the lifestyle of a dog musher and the race's effect on the dogs and all kinds of things. That first one I remember came from a professor at the junior college I was attending in Bethel and I helped him with it when I was in school there. Probably the most important thing we found was that the best chance for success in the Iditarod stemmed from mushers having money, or resources, to prepare. They had good sponsors and good finances. Another thing was that they had not recently been divorced. I assume that was a peace-of-mind thing.

The best Iditarod mushers were stable in their home life. Finances may have been their biggest concern going into the race. Smoking cigarettes and drinking alcohol were big negatives. If someone relied on cigarettes and booze too much it affected them. The more money a musher had the less stress he had on the trail. Mushers who came from the villages to compete had more stress in their lives. That may have been marital discord, too, but it definitely related to subsistence living, whether they were filling the freezer or not, or had money. The cost of flying to Anchorage for the start with the dogs was extremely high. It was almost as if the mushers from rural Alaska had more pressure on them to win or place high to cover costs with prize money, so they could not afford to finish out of the money.

Things I learned by reading that study was that if I was going to do well in the Iditarod I had to find the money to do it, keep a stable home life, and that I was going to have to take care of me. I didn't see how a person could be an alcoholic, with a large amount of liquor in his bloodstream, and do well in the Iditarod, or even just make it across Alaska.

There were a lot of things I liked about being around Iditarod dogs besides being out on the trail by myself in the wind and dark and getting to another village perhaps twenty miles away. Another thing I liked was that the dogs never talked back when you gave them a command. They didn't complain about their food either. I had fun running them. I could run them for five, ten, twenty-five, thirty-five, or fifty miles out of town and the longer I ran the more fun that I had. I always enjoyed running them. For me, the whole Iditarod experience includes the raising, the training, and racing. I liked taking care of them and then seeing their performance after they had been trained.

Without my brothers to help I spent more time alone with the dogs taking care of them. At times I hooked up a dog team and led it into the closest mountains. Some of the best times I had with the dogs involved going out in the wilderness to hunt for moose. Other people took snow-machines, but I took the dogs. After all of my brothers died I did solos for a long time in training in the backcountry and racing. It took a long time to feed them, train them, take care of them, going out fishing for them. It was everything for the dogs.

I really enjoyed that and I know it was good for me. As I said, mushing dogs was my therapy. I like fishing and hunting and I liked being in the outdoors with the dogs. I did it on my own without a training partner. Then I entered the Kusko and my best finish was fourth. I would drive the dogs from Akiak to Bethel to the starting line behind the sled. That was basically their last training. The people of Bethel put on a great race. I've done almost twenty-five of them. They take good care of you and they feed you. They make a big deal about it and they don't skimp. The prize money is good and so a lot of the best mushers in the world come to Bethel at the end of January every year. Jeff King (who has won nine times) and Martin Buser have been there. Paul Gephardt has been there. Lance Mackey has been around. It's a $100,000 purse. Just about every Alaska dog musher wants to try it at least once and a lot of the top ones keep returning.

The Kusko is famous within the state, but not so much outside of the state. I've done about fifteen Iditarods and about twenty-five Kuskos and I think the Kusko is about the best race. The atmosphere is good. Everything is good. You take off from Bethel and head to Kwethluk and then to Akiak. Then you go to Tuluksak and pass through Kalskag and Lower Kalskag to Aniak. You take the tundra route through Whitefish Lake and back through Kalskag to Bethel.

It is interesting to pass through your hometown in the middle of a race. It's always nice to come to Akiak, but it presents some problems. The dogs think they are going home and the race is over. It's a handicap.

After a couple of hundred miles of racing they think it's all over and it's time to go back to the kennel, so I have to fight them a little bit. Their doghouses are right there. They know the way.

I have to force the dogs to go by the kennel. I had a hard time in the beginning, but I learned how to do it successfully over the years. Now they obey me and do whatever I tell them to do so I have them in control. Passing through Akiak I see all of the people I know and my family is cheering for me. My biggest focus is the dogs. I have had dogs flop over in their harnesses because they want to go to their doghouses. They don't want to leave town again, but we're not at the finish line, so they have to go on. When they start flopping over like that I have to go pick them back up. Some of them do it again. They think they're done. Their attitude is, *Forget it. We're home.*

A lot depends on the lead dog and the leaders I have now usually respond. We have little problems going through, but I generally try to go past Akiak at a fast clip and keep them occupied with voice commands. If I get tangled up my relatives will help me sort it out. It's nice to see my human friends, but my dog friends don't really want to keep mushing.

Even when Walter was alive I did the Kusko. We split the dogs up so we could both race. We just enjoyed the Kusko so much it was great to be part of it. It was like playing a big sporting event on your home field, it was that close to us. For a long while running the Kusko, first with Walter and sharing the experience, and then keeping it going for our family, that was my vacation. I took the time off from work or meetings in order to make sure I was in Bethel in January every year.

CHAPTER 10

Over the last five years I have been joined in running the Kusko each January by my son Mike Jr. We have two teams entered. Junior and I worked in the dog yard and then we both ran the 300. It was something special to be out there with Junior. He had a sprint mentality to go fast and I didn't. I wasn't going to go fast.

I let him choose the best dogs from the kennel and I took some of the others. I had done quite a few Iditarods and had experience and he didn't. He took the best dogs, the pick of the kennel, and the first two years I beat him. I beat him with the leftovers from the kennel.

My experience made the difference in not burning the dogs out by going out too fast. He went out fast and tried to come home fast and you can't do that in the Kusko. The first one we did together was in 2009. We planned our races all winter that we were going to enter together. I wanted Junior to learn how to take care of the dogs in a big race and gain a racing education in the Kusko. That was the number one thing.

In the Kusko, you either make it or you crash if you use the wrong strategy. I've seen a lot of the best mushers' teams crash when they were trying to win. For the first two years Junior went out too fast and he crashed. By the third year he had learned and he didn't go out too fast. He trained harder and that year, in 2011, he beat me and he almost won the Kusko altogether. He lost by about a minute to Paul Gephardt.

Just one minute was the margin that he lost by and if Mike had not stayed too long in Tuluksak he would have got him. Gephardt was twenty minutes ahead out of Tuluksak and Mike made up all of that time to Bethel. When they came onto Front Street in Bethel he was gaining on Paul. But he couldn't quite catch him. It is one of the closest races in Kusko history. Myron Angstman once beat George Attla by less than twenty seconds. I think that was in 1983.

The Kuskokwim 300 has always been big for us. It is big in Akiak, in Bethel, and all throughout the region. It is the hometown race so everyone wants to win it. But it's also the best race in many ways. Mike Jr. has done well and being the competitor he is I think it is our realistic goal for him to win the race one day.

My first Iditarod was in 1992. I finished in forty-first place in 14 days, 8 hours, 46 minutes. The winner that year was Martin Buser and he finished in 10 days, 19 hours, 17 minutes. He won by a lot. Of course, I had been aware of the Iditarod from the time it started in 1973. But there is a pretty big difference between flying to Anchorage to enter the Fur Rendezvous for three days of local racing and flying into Anchorage with a dog team and setting out on the trail for a thousand miles. It cost a lot of money to prepare an Iditarod team. In 1992, I had the dogs and I felt strongly it was time to do it. I had always wanted to do it, so I signed up.

When I entered the Iditarod I thought I would do it and once would be enough. I wanted to do it just to say that I did it. Entering the first time I just wanted to see if I could make it to Nome. If I made it, fine. I thought I had a general idea of what it took to race in the Iditarod. I think I planned five years for my first Iditarod. In 1991, I got the idea to start collecting signatures that were pledges for sobriety. Before I ever carried pledges in the Iditarod I did it in the Kusko 300. My goal was to get 300 signatures for 300 miles. When I started asking people I did not know how they would react and there were some people who said, "No, I don't want to do that." But my goal was one signature per mile and I did that.

Help to obtain signatures came from the Alaska Native Sobriety Movement Council and my friend Greg Nothstine. We gathered pledges of sobriety. All of the ones that I gathered I collected in Bethel. There was no Facebook back then. I had a piece of paper that I showed people that said, "I commit to stay sober for one year. That is my commitment." And I told them I would carry those signatures in my sled as a symbol. The first time I made my 300 signatures. That was the beginning.

It made me feel as if I was doing something good. It made me feel as if I was starting something and paying back for all that crap I went through. I thought it was time to pay back against alcohol, that it was time to advocate for sobriety. It was time to make changes and here's what I did to try to make a change.

I put mileage on my dogs over a period of winters. I didn't just build them up one winter for the Iditarod. I had done the Kusko, so I knew what a hard race could be like, even if it was only three hundred miles instead of a thousand. Yes, it is shorter, but you go faster. There are different things to plan for on the trail. In some ways the Kusko is a harder race than the Iditarod because you go so fast. The Iditarod can be easy if you have a strategy and stick to it. You rest more. You go six hours, rest six hours, go six hours and rest six hours. You definitely have more rest if you are not fighting for the lead. I didn't really know that before the Iditarod, but I found out by doing it.

In those days the maximum size of a team was twenty dogs. That was before it was cut to sixteen dogs. I came into Anchorage with my team. Leading up to the race I was nervous and stressed—as usual. I was like most rookies are. I had too much of everything I was trying to load into my sled. I had too much stuff, but not enough of the right things. My equipment wasn't really prepared properly. I had food and clothing in the sled. I thought I had everything I needed, but that wasn't the case.

When I decided to enter the Iditarod in 1992 I thought I would carry as many pledges for sobriety as I could gather along with me on the trail. This was after my brothers had died in the war on alcohol and I thought I could gain some attention for that cause. When you seek the help of others in order to race, or you get them involved and committed, it makes it just that much harder to scratch if something happens to you on the trail. You are not racing only for you, but for them, too. This time the signatures came from all over the state. I gathered signatures at the Alaska Federation of Natives convention. I gathered signatures at other Native meetings. I think I did so at the National Congress of American Indians. Everywhere I went I collected signatures.

I hit the majority of those special Native meetings and I did it at tribal meetings, too. I gathered pledges everyplace. In Anchorage, I went into the hospitals and anywhere else I could get. I had Greg Nothstine and the Native Sobriety Movement Council helping me. There were regional representatives from around the state and I had them help me.

When I set off for Nome that first time I was carrying pledges of sobriety, I actually had 60,000 signatures with me. I don't know how many pages it was, but the list weighed about ten pounds. It was ten pounds of paper. The funny thing was that all of the top contenders were trying to lighten their loads in the sled and trying to toss out anything to cut their weight and I eagerly added ten pounds.

I took off at the start of the 1992 Iditarod with a race sled that wasn't big enough. It was carrying my sleeping bag, food, snowshoes. I had everything in there except I didn't have enough room to put any dogs in the basket if they needed to be dropped because of weariness or injury. At least in the beginning before I started using up supplies I wouldn't have room for a dog.

Although the Iditarod was a big event the crowds did not seem as large as they were for the Rondy. The start of each was in Anchorage and I thought there were bigger crowds for Fur Rendezvous. Those were the days when you actually mushed out of Anchorage at the start of the Iditarod, racing instead of it just being a ceremonial start. We raced all of the way from downtown Anchorage to Eagle River. There was a lot of punchy snow, not smooth. The twenty or so miles counted back then. There were a lot of people downtown and lining the Glenn Highway into Eagle River. We ate there and then packed up the dogs quickly and held the restart in Wasilla four hours later. It was too rushed in Eagle River and hurrying to Wasilla. Besides the ceremonial start in Anchorage, that's why they now have the re-start in Willow or Wasilla on the next day. I think it was really stressful for the dogs and it was for me. You had four hours to get ready and then truck out to Wasilla. You had to feed the dogs in between.

Wasilla was a whole 'nother start the next day. My start in Wasilla was very good, comfortable. It was good to get away from crowds and start into the true wilderness, leaving all of the hoopla behind. It really was good to get the hell out of there and away from any distractions. When we took off from Wasilla it was a relief. Everything else was behind me and all I had to do was mush.

That relaxed feeling didn't last very long, though. I got out to the Rabbit Lake area and the terrain was treacherous. My dogs hated that punchy snow and I had to drop three dogs at Rabbit Lake. They got injured. I left behind one lead dog and two team dogs. That punchy show damaged their shoulders. It was another tough experience. The discouraging thing was that we were only at the beginning of the race.

Right away I had to haul those three dogs off of the bad trail from Rabbit Lake to Skwentna. When I got to Skwenta I was tired of trying to manage those three unruly dogs when there was really no room in the sled for them. It was kind of a nightmare. It was a very rough trail and by the time I reached Skwentna I was totally exhausted and dehydrated. And this is right away in the race, the first hundred miles or so. It was a shaky start for me.

Since I didn't feel well and I had to regroup with my dogs I declared my twenty-four-hour layover at Skwentna. The race has changed in recent years and mushers go much further down the trail before declaring their twenty-four. But back then there were plenty of other mushers in Skwentna to spend time with. Joe Garnie, Norman Vaughan, Joe Redington, Vern Cherneski, and Tim Mundy were all there hanging out with Joe Delia. As usual, Joe Delia's hospitality for mushers was great.

I was using an OT Sled and the screws had come off so my sled was damaged beyond repair. I needed a twenty-four break to replace it. Joe Delia was working on my sled. Tim Mundy scratched right there. I got to know Joe Redington, Vern, and Joe Garnie during that daylong break.

It was a really discouraging time because I was trying to fix that sled and I couldn't do it. It was all shot. The screws wouldn't stay in.

Tim Mundy had a Tim White—made white toboggan sled. I tried to make a deal with Tim Mundy then. I told him what was happening with my sled and since he was out of the race I asked if he would trade with me. At first he was reluctant. I said, "Tim, I want to continue in the race, but I don't have a sled. My sled is gone." After a while he agreed to the trade. He said, "I agree. With that toboggan you'll have a chance to make it to Nome."

So we switched and I moved all my gear into the bigger toboggan. From then on things went well. The toboggan sled was quite good going over the rough parts at Rohn and the Dalzell Gorge. It was a pretty sturdy sled and it hung in there.

That year Joe Garnie lost his team. He was ahead of me, but traveling between Finger Lake and Rainy Pass he hit a tree. It snapped his dogs off their lines. I caught up to him at Rainy Pass. He was sitting there with his sled and the dogs weren't there. Joe Redington lost his team, too, and I caught up to him as well. Joe Redington hit his head on a tree branch and was separated from his team. Joe was walking along the trail and I offered him a ride. He was sweating and he said that he would walk because if he rode on a sled he would freeze. He declined the ride and I caught up to his dogs about fifteen miles from Rainy Pass. I secured his dogs so they couldn't run off again. When I got into Rainy Pass I told folks there what happened with Joe and where his dogs were. I told them that they needed to go back and look for Joe and they took off on snow-machines. They zoomed out of there.

In the early part of that race it was minus forty degrees. It was cold. It was something. But I still had seventeen dogs after the fiasco when I dropped that group in Skwentna. It stayed cold and even got colder. I hardly slept all of the way to Ruby. I had difficulty sleeping in check-points. I hardly slept on the trail, but that's what everyone says. It is a race of sleep deprivation. Boy was I tired when I got into Ruby, a little more than five hundred miles into the race on the northern route. I didn't really take good care of myself. I was dehydrated. I was wiped out in the Ruby Hills and when I got to Ruby I was exhausted. I was staggering around. No one wants to scratch from the Iditarod, but there are low points along the trail when you are hungry and tired and wonder what you are doing. It happens every time. You have to fight through it or you might quit the race. Then you will regret it later.

In Ruby I felt terrible. But Joe Garnie and Joe Redington were there and they helped me. They boosted my spirits. They kept saying, "You can do it! You can do it!" But I was so tired and staggering around dehydrated some people actually thought I had relapsed, gone to the Ruby liquor store and bought some whiskey. They thought I was drunk. People said, "Mike Williams is drunk. He is mushing for sobriety and he's drunk." I was so tired that I looked like that.

Carrying those signatures motivated me all of the way. I was never going to quit. I needed sleep. Emmitt Peters, the 1975 Iditarod winner, is from Ruby and he was there. He told me, "Get some sleep. Get some sleep." So in Ruby, for the first time since the race started I had a good three, four hours sleep. Then I got myself hydrated. I had some food. I was like a new man. I woke up and felt totally different. I had energy.

Once I left Ruby refreshed and was on my way to Galena things went very well. Charlie Boulding was in Galena and that was the first time I ever met him. I started talking to him. Good guy. He won the Yukon Quest twice. Edgar Nollner, who had been part of the 1925 Serum Run when mushers delivered the life-saving diphtheria medicine to Nome because airplanes were grounded, came to see me. That was both inspiring and funny in a way. I was sleeping in Galena and as I woke up I could tell some Elders of the community were looking at me. One of them was Edgar. At the time he was eighty-seven years old and he was the last surviving member of the Serum Run. When I saw him I thought I was still asleep and dreaming. But he said a nice thing. He compared my carrying of the sobriety pledges to Nome to his carrying the medicine to Nome. Lives were at stake immediately when Edgar carried the medicine. I felt an obligation to finish the race for those pledging their sobriety. If I failed, they might fail, too. Maybe in my own way I was carrying life-saving medicine to Nome also.

Besides Edgar, Sidney Huntington, one of the Elders of Galena was there, too. They saw how wiped out I appeared. They both looked at me and said, "Mike, get some damned sleep. You need to go to bed." So I had a good rest in Ruby and I had a good rest in Galena—I got more sleep.

I had fun with Charlie Boulding. That year he was just running a team of yearlings to get them ready for an Iditarod challenge up front. He told good stories about the Quest. And Edgar and Sidney were looking out for me and they had good advice about sleeping.

I regrouped and got stronger with all of that rest. I started to feel like I knew what I was doing. The dogs had good rest, too, and they perked up and wanted to go. I started eating well at the checkpoints and taking care of myself. After that I traveled with Charlie and we had so much fun laughing. We had a good time on the way to Nome. During that stretch from Ruby on is where I started understanding how to take care of myself on the Iditarod Trail and getting the hang of resting the dogs. I did the race in fourteen days, which was not bad at that time. Charlie Boulding really encouraged me along the way. He also shared his food. He had beaver meat and I did not. But he shared his stuff with me and we just had a good time all the way into Nome to the finish line.

When I got to Unalakleet, where the route turns toward the Bering Sea, I got a very big welcome from that Eskimo village. The people really took care of me in that community. They came out for me and gave me Eskimo food—*muktuk,* or whale meat. That was special. They were glad to see me and I had a very happy stay in Unalakleet. They were very aware of me being the one who was carrying the signatures making the pledges for sobriety. They responded to that.

Along the way in the villages many individuals came up to me and said, "Mike, I'm glad you're doing this." Some of them were intoxicated and they said, "I'm having a little trouble with drinking, too. I'm glad you're doing it and I support you." Although they were drinking at the time. But the next year when I did the race and went through there I would see some of the same people and they said, "Mike, I've been sober for six months. I decided to sober up and I just wanted to let you know that your influence is something that is changing my life." I had some of those testimonials along the trail about people becoming sober and that really told me that what I was doing was worth doing and it motivated me.

When I got to Safety, which is only twenty-two miles from Nome, I knew I was going to finish. I had had my doubts during the early part of the race. I had made mistakes. But I had straightened myself out and got stronger as I went on. I had faith and I was going to make it. From Safety on, it was tears all of the way to Nome. I was going to make it and I was thinking about my brothers and what they had gone through. I was doing it for them and with them and it was just really emotional.

The last stretch of the race is on Front Street in Nome and going up I was nearly overcome with emotion. Finishing the Iditarod was something I had accomplished and it was the greatest feeling, to get to the finish line, having achieved a goal, and with those 60,000 signatures. I was sad about the loss of my six brothers, but I was happy carrying the hope for the 60,000. That's what I was doing it for and people came out from the bars and someone shouted, "Ahhhh!" not really making sense. And I said, "That's the reason I'm mushing, because of that guy. That guy can change his life and that's why I'm going to continue to do it. He is drinking right now, but I have hope for him. That's why I'm mushing the Iditarod, for that guy."

I knew as soon as I finished my first Iditarod I was going to do it again. It was an accomplishment to get to Nome on the first run, with a lot of challenges from the beginning of the race. But I learned as I went and it got better and better as I rested smarter and took care of myself. I really enjoyed it as the race went on. I earned the belt buckle. It was a special achievement, partially because of all of the trials and tribulations. Also because of all of the people I met along the trail, and the mushers I got to know and traveled with. It was special to see what the dogs could do. When I got to Nome it was a great feeling. I thought about it and felt, *Maybe I can continue to do better next year and maybe into the future. If I can keep doing it and continue to collect the signatures, do the advocacy, it's all worth doing.*

CHAPTER 11

After finishing the Iditarod I gave the 60,000 pledges to the Sobriety Movement Council. They took them to keep in the records. I had already decided that I was going to keep racing in the Iditarod and that meant that I would keep gathering signatures for sobriety.

I was not sure how many I could obtain every year, but I didn't think I could get 60,000 each time. I went into each Iditarod season with the goal of collecting 50,000 each year. And I did average about 50,000 for a while. It might not seem like there are enough people in Alaska, given that there were about 600,000 people in the entire state at the time. Some people kept signing year after year, I guess. They looked at it as renewing a vow or something, one year at a time.

We all know that the recovering alcoholic looks at his situation as one day at a time, so why not one year at a time on the pledges? I spent a lot of time getting those signatures. Wherever I went I took the papers. Maybe it's like selling books when you give talks or go to conferences. I did it consistently for three straight Iditarods. I competed in those Iditarods, but it cost too much money and I had to stop for a while and pay my bills. I finished thirty-first in 1993 and I finished twenty-eighth in 1994.

That was one of my best finishes. I did not race in 1995 or 1996 because I was working hard raising money for my family.

When I came back to the race in 1997 I placed eighteenth and that was my best finish ever. I had another good race in 1998 when I finished twenty-third. And I was twenty-third again the next year. I placed in the top thirty again in 2000, finishing twenty-eighth. Prize money was being paid for the top thirty. Between 2001 and 2005 I raced every year, but my placings began dropping into the thirties and it was getting too expensive to go every year. I skipped 2006. It was hard to stay away and I returned in 2007 and finished thirty-ninth.

I was also getting older, advancing into my late fifties, and on the cusp of turning sixty, so I was getting a little bit slower. When I did the race in 2009 I finished forty-second. The other factor was that Mike Jr. had been working hard in the dog yard all of those years and it was time for him to take over the team for the Iditarod, too, not just race in the Kuskokwim 300. Junior was a rookie in 2010 and he did a great job. He finished twenty-sixth in his first Iditarod. It was pretty obvious it was time for him to take over for the old man. He keeps getting better. He finished thirteenth in 2011, better than I ever did. Now our roles are pretty much reversed. I help him train the dogs and he races the best dogs of the kennel in the Iditarod.

In 2012 Mike made a bigger breakthrough and finished eighth overall. That puts him within reach of the top. I was very proud of him. I am very proud of him. In 2013 I went back to the Iditarod. It was one of my goals as a father to run the Iditarod with my son. We both ran that year—and that was very expensive to do. Mike did not have one of his best races. He finished twenty-third and I finished forty-fifth. That may have been my farewell race. I may be retired from the Iditarod. It's Mike's turn to represent the family now and he is doing a great job. He had a very difficult race in 2014 when some dogs got sick and he ran short-handed for a long time, but still finished eleventh. That was a great achievement.

One thing about living in a village like Akiak off the Alaska road system, it makes it much more expensive to get goods and services. And it makes it much more expensive to be a musher and have dogs. It costs a lot more money to ship things to a village from Anchorage after it has already been shipped to Anchorage from someplace else. My first three years doing the Iditarod we had to limit the family budget. We weren't making big money anyway and Maggie and I had to limit our spending. We had to depend more on fish and game to eat than store-bought food than we ordinarily did. We had to be lean and mean at home to run the Iditarod.

My family was behind me. I was sober. I was strong and getting stronger. They supported that life without alcohol and my work advocating for sobriety. I was doing something positive. They supported that. My wife supported that. Everybody supported what I was doing. But when I started competing in the Iditarod I really didn't know how expensive it would be. I knew it was costly, but with transportation and food for the dogs, it was more than I thought. At the time I didn't care so much about the finances because it was part of my healing process and I needed to take on that challenge to make me a stronger person and to make me healthy. I had to do something meaningful for my brothers who were all in their graves. I had to do something in their memory. It was something that made me feel good to accomplish and it was worthwhile to do for our people.

I was fortunate that I did not have to start from scratch. We already had good dogs that had been in the family, so I did not have to buy a team and start training from the bottom. But you have to fly the team to races and to the start of the Iditarod and bring them home from Nome. Just to get to Fourth Avenue for the start and be prepared and ready to race it costs at least $50,000 for an Iditarod race. Then we want to fly the family to Nome to see the finish and it costs maybe $800 to $1,000 per person. Then to get Alaska Airlines to move the team from Nome to Bethel is about $3,000.

As much as we rely on fish we catch from the Kuskokwim River, you still have to feed the dogs high-caliber dog food and meat. They need the nutrients and that costs a good sum—not only buying the food, but shipping it to Akiak.

What I did by entering the Iditarod and staying involved was become part of a community of dog mushers, a fraternity, a family. We are all part of the same big event and although we don't all live near one another when we see each other away from the race over the rest of the year we relate to one another, give each other hugs and ask about our immediate families. You get to know people you wouldn't otherwise know and you have the Iditarod in common.

Being an Iditarod racer, especially one that keeps coming back, makes you part of the Iditarod event and history. The same way that the Iditarod becomes part of your life, you become part of the Iditarod. The mushers compete against each other, but they also support each other. We help each other out on the trail when it is needed. It is us against the elements and sometimes the elements would get to be too much if we didn't help each other. Like if someone's dog team gets away.

When we are not on the trail we have a lot in common when we see each other. Since everyone lives in different places we only periodically see one another the rest of the year, particularly in large groups, but when we do it's like a family reunion. One good part of the Iditarod for me has been the friendships formed with people like DeeDee Jonrowe and other folks. Since the time I was involved in the Iditarod I have been going to churches and not to bars and I spend time with different people. I believe I have been inside a bar two times in the last fifteen or twenty years.

That is in all of the time I have been sober. Those times were going in to bars with friends. Once was in Nome with Hugh Neff. We went into the Polaris and I drank sodas. And another time it was the Board of Trade, also in Nome after an Iditarod. It reminded me about the smell of booze and the smell of smoke and how there were a lot of other positive things to do instead of sitting in a bar such as attending a reindeer feed, going to church or meetings. There are a lot of other activities to spend your time on.

There are Natives that wanted to feed me their food instead of me going out to drink if I am in a place where alcohol is permitted. The Eskimos in the area wanted to feed me an Iñupiat spread. From the first time I did the Iditarod I had a great reception in the villages, tons of kids, tons of Elders who came over and wanted to talk to me. Sometimes I think some of the other mushers don't spend enough time with the people in the villages. But the people in the villages came to see me. There were crowds in the checkpoints.

Of course that first year they all knew I was carrying the signatures for sobriety. They helped make me feel that I was doing something positive and influencing change for the better in people. The goal was to just change the life of one person. If I did that, it was enough. If I saved one life.

Right after finishing my first Iditarod I felt a sense of accomplishment, but I started thinking I wanted to do it again and do it in a better way, finishing in a shorter amount of time. I think a lot of first-time finishers think that way. For me, it was especially true because I had been traveling with such a great group of mushers like Charlie Boulding, Joe Garnie, and Joe Redington. Just being around them inspires you to want to do better. What a great group of men.

Charlie Boulding became one of my best friends. Over the years I would borrow dogs from him when he had extra dogs from the Iditarod. After that first race I would stay with Vern Cherneski in Big Lake and so did Charlie. We would have moose soup together. There was a bond formed with mushers in that first race of mine.

At this point I can run the Kusko in my sleep, but the Iditarod was something else. There was always something different, a new challenge. Over time I became identified with the signatures and that was OK. I became Mike Williams, the Iditarod musher who mushes for sobriety. It evolved after the first time. It was also clear from the way the kids in the villages came out to see me that they were starved for Native heroes. They need positive roles models. That's what I think Joe Garnie was. That's what I became. John Baker even more so after he won the 2011 Iditarod. These kids really look up to John Baker. Joe Garnie changed his life, too, moving away from alcohol. John Baker became a champion. These kids need heroes. They need more in their lives than looking around and seeing someone who is a woman beater, or people abusing alcohol and drugs. It is very important to give them something positive.

You gain a lot doing the Iditarod once. You see where you made mistakes. You learn how it works and what it is like being out there in the wilderness in the race. When I came back for my second Iditarod I was definitely more knowledgeable. After having seen it and experiencing the trail you have an idea what's going on. I was better prepared ahead of time, too, with the equipment in the sled. I had the right stuff and supplies. I planned ahead more about taking better care of myself so

I would not get dehydrated. I had more food for the dogs and I brought dog coats for protection if it was extremely cold. I also carried fresh signatures pledging sobriety.

Right after my first Iditarod I made a report to the Alaska Federation of Natives along with the sobriety council. We gave them the numbers of signatures acquired and told them what we did promoting sobriety. They applauded what we did and they thought it was the right thing to do. They liked the idea of being proactive and agreed it was a good idea to lobby other Native organizations and educational organizations to make their meetings alcohol free.

We were successful in making the Alaska Federation of Natives convention alcohol free, unlike during other years. I think that led to the Association of Alaska School Boards passing a resolution supporting sobriety effort activities, stressing positive leadership without any alcohol influence. I believe that has made a huge difference making people conscious of their alcoholic intake. It was not a mandate, but voluntary. People seemed to take it up that it was a good thing to have sober leadership because we needed to have positive role models.

The first year we gathered 60,000 signatures, but I think for my second Iditarod we collected about 100,000 pledges. That was a one-time thing. All of the attention that I got the first year helped and other organizations threw themselves into it to gather the signatures of people making the pledge to stay sober for one year. I am sure that many of the names were the same as the first year, but that was OK, it was another year. Do we know how many of those people stayed sober for a year? No. But hopefully, by signing their name this made them at least think about it and try to be sober.

We branched out in the collection of signatures. It went all through the villages, to Native organizations, to nonprofit organizations all throughout Alaska. We made that effort. We stepped up our efforts not only throughout Alaska, but in the Lower 48 at tribal meetings. We got a lot of those pledges in the Lower 48. We also resumed collecting the signatures early on and didn't wait for the fall to start doing it. I think we got started in April, just a month after the Iditarod ended. We spent most of a year doing it. We raised money through the Alaska Federation of Natives for Greg Nothstine to travel throughout the state and to make speeches along with other board members from the AFN sobriety movement.

Greg is a great athlete who has won a large number of medals at the World Eskimo-Indian Olympics and he also carried the banner of WEIO. When he traveled to the Bush to speak about sobriety he also gave demonstrations of the blanket toss. The blanket toss revolves around a sealskin blanket and got its start as a way to celebrate a successful hunt. When the hunting party was successful one man was lifted on the blanket and thrown in the air to see how high he could go. But he could not do it on his own. The men, or pullers, who surround the blanket, pull it tight and they are as much a part of the jump as the one person in the middle. For Greg, this was not only a colorful way to get people's attention, but something with a double meaning through a traditional activity alongside the speech for sobriety. The message that Greg was sending was that when you're healthy, when you work together, when you pull together, it makes the blanket toss work. If the pullers don't work together simultaneously, and there are not enough people pulling, the blanket toss will be a failure.

I was starting to become involved with various government boards where I could also carry the message. I have been on the school board in Akiak for thirty-five years and I served on the state board of education for eight years and have had four terms on the Association of Alaska School Boards. I was on some boards then and I have been on several boards since.

By carrying the pledges in my first Iditarod I got some attention for sobriety. The second year we spread the movement in a much bigger way. People began to know me that way. I think by the third year I carried signatures in the Iditarod, the label was on me as the musher for sobriety. Especially by the third year people knew what I was doing and were very interested. I received compliments from many organizations and I was having stories written about me in the newspaper. The attention helped. The focus on sobriety helped.

CHAPTER 12

I went into my second Iditarod with more confidence and more preparation. I knew I was going to get more sleep and understood better how to take care of the dogs. I trained the dogs better and I came to the Anchorage area in advance and stayed at Vern Cherneski's house in Big Lake.

That way I didn't have to fly me and the dogs to Anchorage close to the race and feel rushed. We went to the Mat-Su Valley a month before the race. Vern had competed in the Fur Rendezvous for years and the Iditarod, so he knew what I was doing. We had a place to stay, a wonderful home, and we trained out of his yard, where we had access to the Iditarod Trail.

I could take the dogs right out onto the trail and mush to Skwentna or Finger Lake. That was a huge difference in preparation. I ended up staying with Vern about ten times before Iditarods. It was such a big plus. Dog mushing is so big and popular in the Valley I was lucky to have somebody, to have people that wanted to help. There was a woman there named Annabelle and she helped us, too. She loaned me a dog truck to take the team to the starting line in Anchorage.

Between all of that help and better planning I was much better prepared. I had a place to stay, a way to train, and I did my food drops putting together the bags for the checkpoints in the Valley. I could buy many of the things I needed in Anchorage, which was cheaper than Akiak, and I didn't have the extra cost of shipping my food drops from Akiak to Bethel to Anchorage. Everything was smoother all around and I began to develop a smoother operation.

I think experience and preparation are keys to success in the Iditarod. You have to plan ahead and prepare. I think people like Rick Swenson and DeeDee Jonrowe have got it down to a science. They are so organized and efficient. They bring just so much meat and chicken and commercial feed for the dogs. You have to be really efficient in each checkpoint, and that includes packing the bags right in the first place. If you are going to be a contender to win the Iditarod, you have to be very fast in the checkpoints. You can make up a lot of time there or lose a lot of time.

One thing I was smart enough to do that I didn't do the first year was to ship an extra sled to McGrath. During the first part of the race you need a tougher sled to get through the Dalzell Gorge and get to Rainy Pass. After that the trail is smoother and less rugged and you gain by switching to a lighter, faster sled. If you are going to bust up a sled the chances are high it will happen in the early part of the race, so if you ship a second sled out it can help in an emergency. It was a plus.

It was terrific going through the villages. People were more aware of what I was doing carrying the sobriety pledges and why I was running. Men, women, and children came out from their homes to greet me in every checkpoint and they encouraged me to continue the race. They thanked me for doing what I was doing. Those continuous testimonials from people really encouraged me. I saw some individuals I had seen on the Iditarod Trail my first year who said they were drinking and they were going to try and stop. The second year when I saw them some of them told me they weren't drinking anymore.

There was also a little bit of a homecoming when I passed through Shageluk. Shageluk is not very far from Akiak and neither is Anvik. I have a bunch of relatives there. One great-grandfather was from Holy Cross. There was a good reception from relatives in that area. They were aware of what I was doing. I had had prior contact with the tribal councils in those places and I had traveled to them when I was a mental health worker. Those villages had experienced some rage because of alcohol.

For the most part I was traveling alone in this Iditarod. Even though I spent some time with those guys in the checkpoints the year before I liked to mush by myself. I didn't want to get into other people's plans and issues and problems. I had enough of my own, so I preferred focusing on my own race and not traveling with anyone else. The first race I was woozy in some checkpoints and not doing well physically. This year was much better. My first year I wanted to get to Nome. This time I wanted to get to Nome in as short a time as was possible. The first race had to do with survival. This race was racing, trying to do the best I could, not just finish.

It was still hard. There is never an easy year on the Iditarod. It's still a thousand miles long and there is still snow and ice and wind and weather. I spent some time in the checkpoints or nearby on the trail with Terry Adkins from Montana, who was the first Iditarod veterinarian before he started racing; Dewey Halverson, who finished second in 1985 to Libby Riddles; Mark Nordman, who became the Iditarod race marshal; Bob Holder; and Jason Barron.

That year the weather was good along the trail until we got to White Mountain. It was only seventy-seven miles from the finish line and we had to take a mandatory eight-hour rest. But then a blizzard blew in from the Bering Sea and changed everything. We were held up in White Mountain. Nobody could go and more and more mushers came in. They ended up calling us the Gang of Seventeen because we all followed one another down the trail to Nome.

The money places had all been decided so it was determined that we would not race against each other, just help each other by traveling in a single line. The late Jerry Austin organized the whole thing so we could finally get to the finish line and not just be stuck in White Mountain.

Jerry Austin was the leader of the pack. He was just like John Wayne. He led the charge from White Mountain to Nome and it was a sight to see going in, a train coming from White Mountain, one dog team after another. Everyone finished within minutes of one another. They opened the finish chute wide and ran us through. When the dog lot filled up they just had teams parked along the side of Front Street. It was the middle of the night, too, when we got there. The whole thing looked a little bit crazy and there has never been anything like it in the Iditarod. That was before the rules changed to pay prize money to the top thirty finishers. If it had still been in the era of payouts to just the top twenty, I wonder what would have happened. Maybe it would have been a free-for-all.

That year I got to know a lot more mushers because we were all stuck in White Mountain together for so long. I had known Jerry Austin because he had consistently run the Kusko. He won the 300 in 1981 and 1982. I first traveled with Jerry in the Kusko in 1983 when I was a rookie. I placed seventh and took rookie of the year.

In that Iditarod I remember traveling with Kathy Tucker, Diana Moroney, and Bob Holder through the blizzards. I remember resting my team out of Golovin because we couldn't go through the drifts of snow. It was very hard. Bob and Kathy and I sat around for a while resting the dogs in the middle of the blizzard. We rested for two or three hours and decided to go again.

Between Elim and White Mountain that year we were stuck for hours and hours. I remember going with Dewey and Mark Nordman and we had to break a lot of trail, including in the Elim hills. I applauded my leaders for working so hard to break trail. The snow was two or three feet deep in some places and there was no trail. It was blown over. But we took turns and I was part of that trail-breaking crew.

In White Mountain Terry Adkins organized a poker game. Some others were drinking. Everybody was twiddling their thumbs, though, ready to take off. We fed our dogs and rested and then we waited. We were waiting for a trail to be put in so we could move. There was so much snow. Lynda Plettner was a character and always made us laugh in the checkpoints. Terry was pretty much an Elder of the Iditarod.

Jerry and Terry were the most experienced mushers in the group. Mostly when Jerry stopped we stopped. When he went, we went. People said it was like a wagon train in the Old West. Some mushers wanted to go ahead, but Jerry pretty much kept everyone in line. But there was no money to be had at that point. The money had been decided, but there was still the spirit of racing and some mushers wanted to finish higher. I got to know Mark Nordman and Diana Moroney better and they were some of the nicest people on the trail.

In Nome we came roaring down Front Street. Leo Rasmussen, who was mayor of Nome and president of the Iditarod Trail Committee, was the checker. There we came, one, two, three, four, five, ten, eleven, twelve, sixteen, seventeen of us. It was something. I finished thirty-first overall. I've never seen anything like that finish before—nobody had. I'll never see it again.

If you look at the standings there was a two-day gap between twenty-first place and twenty-second when Dave Olesen finished five seconds ahead of Jerry and there was a seven-minute gap between Dave and Peryll Kyzer in thirty-eighth.

There was a lot of snow at the end of the race that year. I think traveling with that group and finishing together solidified my wanting to do the race again. The first and second years I did the race on a minimum budget. We had very little. It was a very tight budget. The next time the last seventy-seven miles was determined by the weather and I still wanted to race to Nome.

So I entered the Iditarod again in 1994. Gathering signatures had become an ongoing project with a lot of help. I couldn't gather so many by myself. I don't remember exactly, but I think that year we had 80,000 pledges for sobriety. In three years it had reached something like 200,000 signatures. That was a lot of people saying they were committing to sobriety. They all did not make it for a year, of course. If alcohol was so easy to beat, just by writing your name, a lot more people would be sober. But it's an addiction and it's hard to stop drinking. We all know that.

Some people should never drink. They are alcoholics. I understand that some people can drink in moderation and not be in harm's way. They might have a beer in a bar after work with friends. They might drink a glass of wine with dinner. I am not against drinking in moderation like that. If you are in control, if you are not overdoing it, that is one thing. That's fine for some people. But some people have to cut it off altogether and be 100 percent sober.

What we have seen in rural Alaska, though, is not moderation. We have seen the evils of alcohol, the misuse of alcohol at its worst, people getting drunk and committing suicide or violence against others. People were getting drunk and going out onto the tundra and falling through the ice on snowmachines or freezing to death. One thing we have in Alaska is a local-option law where the people in a village can vote to be dry or damp or have alcohol. It is difficult to ban alcohol altogether in a community. We saw that tried in the United States during Prohibition and ended up with bootlegging and people going to jail. Prohibition never worked. So you have to wonder about liquor bans when some people would still like to drink and do it in moderation and some people are desperate to drink and find a way to do it.

Alcohol will always be around and it will always be around the villages. It will definitely always be around in Bethel. Jets land in Bethel and it is legal to sell alcohol on those planes. There are bars and liquor stores in Alaska and restaurants that sell alcohol. Alcohol cannot be eliminated, except in villages that are dry. Akiak is dry. Bethel is damp. There are no liquor stores in Bethel now. But you can drink alcohol at home there. You can bring it in from Anchorage and take it home. There are no bars or liquor stores, but you can still drink legally.

Akiak is supposed to be dry. That means you cannot bring alcohol into Akiak. You cannot import it. It is prohibited. The regulations say you cannot import it, but you can possess it at home. How does it get here? The language was put into that local option law that you cannot bring it to Akiak, but you can possess it. It is illegal to carry it off the plane. In the history of that law about importing there has never been a conviction. Enforcement of the law is key and nobody wants to enforce it, including our police. They just look the other way. The law has been on the books for thirty years.

If we have suspicion that alcohol is being imported the Western Alaska Narcotics team can get involved. If we have tips that alcohol is being imported we try to intercept them. Those cases involve people who plan to sell alcohol. If a lady gets off the plane and she has one of those little airline bottles with her nobody is going to search her or prosecute her.

We have been looking at what to do about that, but there has been nobody convicted of bringing alcohol in like that in their coat pocket. In recent times we have started to look at the issue on the tribal level. We have met people at the airport and if we have suspicion we're going to search their bags and take care of them through the tribal court. That has happened. Right now we have three cases.

The tribal council is looking at these cases. A fine can be levied and the ultimate punishment is that the person is banned from Akiak. They are forced to leave and not return to Akiak. It is a ban from the village. This can become a matter of dispute of jurisdiction between the tribe and the state. Right now we are carrying out an order of banishment. The tribe banned one person and in order for that person to come back he has to request a meeting with the tribal council and have his case reviewed. It was done before. I believe two other times. It is possible that someone would want to go to the state to fight the ban, but that has not happened. They didn't fight it.

If you go back in time, under tribal law people were banished for a reason. It was a traditional thing to do here. This goes back way before Alaska became a state in 1959. It was used for other reasons. It is a traditional and customary way of dealing with a problem. In the recent cases over alcohol the person has not fought the ban. There is so much suffering because of alcohol here. There is bootlegging going on and we are trying to get rid of that.

Many years ago, for two reasons I actually recommended that we open a liquor store and bar in Akiak. One was that bootlegging was starting in Akiak because the liquor store in Bethel closed. People like my brother Frank were going to Bethel to buy booze and having accidents and dying. They ended up drowning in the river. There were quite a few people that perished that way when they were drunk. If we had our own liquor store and bar the people would not get killed going to Bethel to buy alcohol. I thought if we legalized it we would eliminate the danger on those trips and we would cut out the bootlegger. We would be providing alcohol for whoever wanted it legally. That doesn't sound like me right now, but at the time I thought it might be better than the alternative. If we had been a white community we probably would have had a liquor store and bar, but we didn't because we were a Native community.

Right now bootleggers live in Akiak. There are bootleggers in the next village. There are bootleggers in Bethel. Bootleggers in Bethel are thriving. I don't know how people put a number on it, but I hear that alcohol is a $6 million industry in Bethel. The airlines and cargo planes are coming in with booze. Orders are placed in Anchorage at stores. I hear that there are forty bootleggers in Bethel, all of them private liquor stores. They are undercover. They don't pay taxes for their bootlegging.

Those are pretty discouraging numbers for someone who believes in sobriety as part of our health. Alcohol will always be available throughout the world, throughout the United States, and in Alaska and Anchorage. Sobriety has to be a choice. It is my choice as a sobriety guy that during my travels throughout Alaska and the United States that I will never have a beer again the rest of my life. It is my choice. That is my choice whether or not alcohol is available where I live, where I work, where I travel. If it is available legally on Alaska Airlines, in Anchorage, people are going to buy it. But not me. They exchange money for beer.

But a lot of bootleggers are making money off the misery of folks. I keep wondering why. I keep thinking why churches and the establishment aren't in favor of legalizing alcohol. It's been on ballots before. Maybe they believe if someone has to break the law to obtain alcohol it makes it harder to drink. We have had discussions on the tribal council about whether or not Akiak should have legal alcohol. It seems as if the discussion is ongoing and the community is split. People who want to legalize alcohol want to eliminate the bootleggers and loss of tax revenue. If alcohol was legal in Akiak there would be an opportunity to sell it and collect taxes to do other useful things with the revenue. We could fund substance abuse treatment with the money collected from the sale of alcohol. That would be one way of using the money.

The battle over alcohol will never end. It is a battle for a lifetime. The price of alcohol that comes from bootleggers costs a huge amount of money. A bottle of whiskey might cost between $80 and $100 for 7.5 milliliters. Right now we could go out and get a bottle in Akiak for eighty bucks. Only no one would sell it to me. They would think I was trying to trap them. But we know who the bootleggers are and we're trying to deal with them in tribal court. We are writing letters to them and will try to adjudicate them.

I could carry those thousands of signatures on the Iditarod Trail, and that was one way to bring attention to the problem of drinking in rural Alaska, but so many other things had to be done and still have to be done, to help people cope with their alcoholism.

CHAPTER 13

My third Iditarod was in 1994 and I finished in twenty-eighth place, my highest finish to that point. I was carrying the sobriety signatures again, but I knew much better what I was doing on the trail, as well. My time was in the twelve-day range, which had lopped off two days from my rookie year.

That year I was quoted in the *Anchorage Daily News* as saying, "I hate to be on the porch watching when the big dance goes by." That year, too, I was the only Eskimo in the race. Ramy Brooks was entered and did well and he is part Athabascan. Chris Converse of Wasilla, a Tlingit, was in the race, but scratched.

Once again I got to know a lot of other mushers and traveled with some of them. It was wonderful traveling again with Bob Holder and Lynda Plettner, but I also spent time in checkpoints and on the trail with Jerry Austin, Bruce Lee, Frank Teasley, and Ramey Smyth. You get to know those guys as you go along and share time together. Plus John and Jason Barron. I visited them a lot. Susan Butcher, Stan Smith, Linwood Fiedler, Robin Jacobson, Vern Halter, Ramy Brooks, and Kate Persons were around me, too, at different times.

Being out on the trail was great and I was much more confident about what I was doing. But in the background I worried about other things. I kept thinking about how much it cost to race in the Iditarod and wonder how I was going to pay my bills. I thought a lot about my family. I knew that after doing three Iditarods I was going to have to take a break. I was focused on my family and the bills that accumulated and I knew I was going to have to get back to working more and spend less time training.

I was counseling again for the health corporation. That was what I liked to do best. I knew that was all for me in the Iditarod, at least for a little while. I could not afford it any longer. I owed people money and I needed to catch up. I told Maggie that I was going to take a break from the Iditarod and that I was going to skip a race even as much as I wanted to run. I also wanted to take care of my family and the debt had piled up for the dogs for three years.

The plan was to take at least a year off until I could catch up financially. I knew I would come back someday, but I wasn't sure when. I did not run in 1995 or 1996. My philosophy in my fund-raising is that if someone gave me one dollar then I could afford one bootie for a dog. I knew as well as anyone else I was running on a shoestring budget. By comparison, some of the other mushers were corporations. I came back in 1997 and I was still pretty much doing all the preparation and training by myself. I continued doing that for all of my Iditarods until sometime in the 2000s, maybe 2005, when the kids were getting older and Mike Jr. got really interested.

Everything was done solely by me. I took care of the dogs. I did the fishing. I did not depend on anyone. I had a little help from family members and in-laws once in a while, but I didn't have a handler, no consistent help. When March of 1995 rolled around and I was not entered in the Iditarod it was hard. I felt empty and I felt I had no purpose. When I was racing as the Iditarod approached I got anxious and excited, but without being part of it I didn't feel that way. But after doing it three years in a row I noticed my wife was happier and the family was happier that I was home. Maggie was more relaxed because I had paid my bills. We had things that we needed. We fixed the porch and put an addition on the house and put a deck in. I enlarged my house. But there were withdrawal pains from missing the race.

Those two years that I missed the Iditarod were emotionally difficult. The Iditarod gets into you. I went to the start and watched, but it was hard on me. I knew those mushers were going to go out and have fun on the trail. And I knew them all. I didn't do the Iditarod, but I still did the Kuskokwim 300 and local races. I still had the dogs and worked with the dogs every day. They were still a big part of my life. Since I did not do the Iditarod I did not carry signatures pledging sobriety from Anchorage to Nome but I stayed active in the sobriety movement. I continued to advocate for sobriety. I worked with the tribes. I didn't lie down and stop. I traveled to the local schools and I was invited to speak in various communities. When I was asked to speak about alcohol and sobriety mostly I told stories about my own life.

They didn't tell me what to say, but they knew I was going to speak about sobriety. I talked about what happened with my brothers and what I went through. Generally, I said that from my standpoint what I was seeing through my lens was that the issues were still the same. The prisons were full of our people. The government is building more jails and throwing our people in them. They get in trouble from alcohol and then they want to commit suicide. That still resonates. People were suffering in the villages in several ways. The numbers of deaths of Natives was so high from suicide, accidents, and even cancer. Studies even showed that more Natives died from cancer than whites in the same age groups or the same places.

There are between 70,000 and 80,000 disenfranchised kids because of the Alaska Native Claims Settlement Act. They're being treated differently because they are not shareholders of the corporations. Underlying everything is that the state does not recognize the existence of the tribes as authorities and their jurisdiction. We cannot take care of the alcohol issue ourselves and they will never support Native rule. We cannot adjudicate the cases properly. We are doing what we can, but the state doesn't recognize it. We're doing it—those three cases I mentioned—and we feel it is our sovereign right. The state is against that. It won't enforce it. They won't be part of it. They are not stopping us. The state has not taken us to court to challenge that yet. They look the other way.

It took two years for me to pay off my bills and it was a good feeling when I ran out of payments. I was refreshed and wanted to do better in the Iditarod. With three Iditarods under my belt I thought I might be able to place higher. I wanted to do my best and have the best finish of my life in my next Iditarod. And that's the way it went. I finished eighteenth in the 1997 race, earning top-twenty money.

Leading up to that race I had some preparation help. My brother-in-law Willie Ekamrak and one of his cousins, Ray Ekamrak, gave me help with the lush fish traps. He helped me with the training of the second team. He raced the Kusko at the same time and helped me consistently on training days. He went in early to Anchorage to help get the dogs ready.

It was a new thing for me to have daily help with the dogs and it made training and just living my life much easier. I was still working and I tried to pay Willie a little bit for his help. The goal was to record a better finish. I trained more. I put more, longer runs on the dogs and had upgraded, better equipment. I gave the dogs more rest on the trail and I had more patience than I did in the beginning. I didn't start out fast, but the dogs seemed to be improving as we went along the trail.

That year the weather was perfect. If I recall, it was perfect all of the way. There were no storms. The sun was shining a lot. The temperature was between minus ten and minus twenty. It was cool and good for the dogs. That time I really enjoyed traveling with Dave Sawatzky. He was a wise old veteran of the Yukon Quest and I did everything he did. Mitch Seavey was there and Ramey Smyth and Paul Gebhardt. We spent a lot of time together on the trail that year, passing one another, and in checkpoints. I didn't go out fast, but I had my fastest time of 10 days, 15 hours, 45 minutes. I stayed patient and moved along well.

Unlike my first three Iditarods the dogs performed well all of the way to Nome. I had my best running times checkpoint to checkpoint and the reception in the villages was even greater. The people wanted me to do better than I had done and so there was a great deal of support. I had moved to the next level, moving up in the standings, in the race;

I had jumped up from placing in the forties and thirties. It was my best race from start to finish and all along the way. I had a real sense of accomplishment and because I won some prize money I broke even financially for the year. For once I didn't go into debt to run the Iditarod.

I moved up ten places from my last finish and that was a good move. I think the two years of laying off and thinking about the race recharged me. It gave me a lot more energy. I gained confidence and I had the dogs which had enough speed, dogs that were tough and better prepared. Everything was pretty good that year. And with my return to the Iditarod I did carry signatures pledging sobriety that year. I think it was 50,000 of them. I was running into more people in the villages during the race that said, "I signed one of those." I was hearing more testimonials that I was doing a good thing by bringing attention to the problems of alcohol in rural Alaska. Some of those people told me they were staying sober year to year.

After a two-year gap of being on the Iditarod Trail that was music to my ears. To hear those folks who hadn't seen me tell me they were sticking with their sobriety pledge made me feel good. It was always good to hear that I had been part of their change of life. Again, that was a good reminder to me that I was doing something positive. When I was out in the wilderness in the race, not a day went by when I didn't think about my brothers. But that was not only on the Iditarod. Every day, it is consistent today, ever since I lost all of them, I think about them every day.

What happened to my brothers because of alcohol continues to motivate me to help people. It continues to motivate me no matter how difficult the issues are. I still think we need to deal with them head-on and to have conversations about problems instead of sweeping them under the rug. You can't have a problem and look the other way. I hate like heck to look the other way and not do anything at all, even if the problem is a major challenge.

Doing the Iditarod in 1997, coming back to it, was all part of the war I had declared on alcohol. I made that commitment to always fight that war during my grief period, so I am going to continue to fight that as long as I am alive and breathing and able to do that.

A lot of the other mushers also told me they supported what I was doing. The other mushers, the competitors, would say, "Mike, I'm glad that you are doing what you're doing. I wish you well." Others would say, "I'm glad you're doing something." They know my story and when they say "I support what you are doing" I know they are telling me the truth. I think it said a lot when the others voted me the most inspirational musher. I had lost my daughter and kept on mushing, but I think the sobriety work I did figured into their minds, too.

Running the Iditarod is the best and to me it is a beautiful experience. Sure, it gets to be difficult when you are super tired and the elements are acting up very powerfully. You can get discouraged, but also sometimes running the Iditarod is a piece of cake compared to the grief I went through losing my brothers and the struggles with alcohol. The trail is beautiful. I try never to get too down and when I do think about my brothers when I am mushing the dogs on the trail, I think that I am not mushing alone out there. When things are not going right I think that the reason I am doing this is "for you suckers." I get mad at my brothers for the wrong choices they made that took their lives and took them away from us. When I feel like quitting or when things are tough on the trail I think of them and it seems like they are looking down at me encouraging me: "Don't quit. Keep going. Heck, you're doing all right." That's the motivation. But most of the time it's a beautiful feeling being out there in the Alaska backcountry with just me and the dogs.

I hope my brothers are not resting in their graves, but turning somersaults in their graves cheering for me. I feel that my brothers are with me and I want to continuously do the Iditarod for them. I want them to be continuously cheering for me. I don't want them resting in peace. I'm not going to let them rest in peace. The heck with that. I want them to continue to work as long as I'm alive. I also consider other mushers to be my brothers now. Raymie Redington is sort of a brother to me. Hugh Neff is, too. He's just like Walter.

Hugh has an attitude that is like Walter's was. It is dogs first and after that he's going to do his best he can with the dogs. Sometimes he will think he has the best dogs in the world and he can be a competitor who thinks, *I have better dogs than you do and I'm going to kick your ass. I'm going to beat you and my goal is not to finish in second place.* When Walter finished in second place, he was pissed off. He didn't like to lose. It was an insult to come in second place. He wanted to win every race and that was his goal going into the race. He wanted to win and that was his motivation.

I am not like that. I don't have that competitive attitude. I am not hard-core. I'm much more civil and too much of a nice guy. Walter's goal was to win. Hugh reminds me a lot of him and so does Joe Garnie. Joe would think he could take care of dogs better than you and bring out a better performance.

The 1997 race was one of my best years running and in the sense of accomplishment, finishing higher in the race. It was also so good to be back in it. It was very special that year. I was more relaxed and less stressed.

By that race, too, I was coming out of my shell from the grief, from having lost so many family members. That is a long healing process and I think in some ways you never heal all of the way and that I am still healing. I'm not completely well, and although a lot of years have passed, it's still fresh in my mind losing all of my brothers. I'm still repairing damage to myself, to the family, and to the community. You never get over it completely, especially when you have lost six people.

That is one reason I am haunted by the young ones who are gone because of suicide or domestic violence. You never get over that. But for me, mushing in the Iditarod Trail Sled Dog Race, and returning to the race when I did in 1997 and doing so well, was very helpful. It was also very healthy for me.

Left: Mike on the sled with the family in the sled.

Below: At the Iditarod starting line getting ready for a 1,000-mile race to Nome.

Above: Living in Akiak, Mike can be a father, grandpa, and uncle without leaving his house since the kids all drop by to visit regularly.

Left: With wife, Maggie.

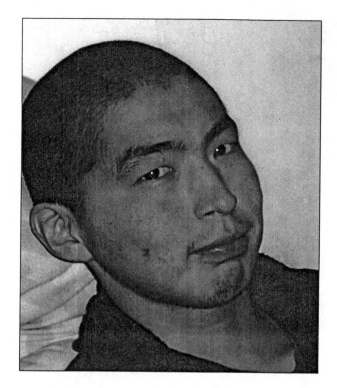

*Mike Williams Jr.,
Mike's son, who has
taken over the family
kennel and become an
Iditarod racer*

One reason the Iditarod is fun for mushers is the great scenery.

Proud parents in Nome with Junior. Mother Maggie is on the left, Iditarod finisher Mike Jr. is in the middle, and Mike Sr. is on the right.

Coming into the finish line in Nome.

Above: Mike in Safety during the 100th-anniversary All Alaska Sweepstakes race that threw attention on the famous annual series of dog-mushing competitions in Nome beginning in 1908 and ending because of World War I.

Left: Mike and Maggie in Nome at the Iditarod finish line.

Whether it is about mushing or important Alaska issues, Mike Williams always has something to say and his opinions are sought.

Mike Williams the politician listening to Gov. Tony Knowles.

CHAPTER 14

There have been dogs in my family for generations, going back I don't-know-how-many years. In the North dogs were always used for work, to help haul wood and water on the sled, for transportation between villages and into the wilderness to help us hunt.

The Alaska husky is not a registered breed, but an offshoot of Siberian huskies and other kinds of dogs. Our people have been dependent on dogs for survival for a long time. Ever since Akiak has been around we have had dogs and the dogs have been there with us. They are our partners in survival. Not all dogs are equal, of course. The best dogs become leaders.

It takes a good build, attitude, and speed to become a leader, especially when you are talking about racing dogs for the Iditarod. We began training them early, as pups. When they were just little guys we let them loose to run behind the team. It was natural for them to follow. The fastest pup has an opportunity to become the best leader.

What we did when the pups were five or six months old is let them run behind the team when we went out to check our traps, were going to the next village, or on a training run. We usually have twenty pups a year in our kennel and we know that all twenty are not going to develop into stars on the Iditarod team.

Another way we train and develop the racing dogs is by raising them in fish camp and over the summer where they are constantly socialized with each other and with humans. They grow up as part of the family with the grandkids. They are petted and held as they are growing up. Then they get those chances to run loose around here. We then try to focus down on ten dogs, the ten pups we think will become the best. In a way they sort themselves out to let us know which ones have potential and which ones will probably not be good enough to make it onto our racing team. By eight months we can usually tell and when we have chosen the top group we give away the other ten to people in the village. There are always people who need or want a dog.

The first training of the dogs is running behind a four-wheeler when it is warmer out and there is no snow. That's when they are broken into harness. We start slowly. They only run two, three, four, and five miles and we constantly watch their speed and their gait. We have a kennel of about fifty dogs, but we cannot afford to have it keep growing and spend the money feeding more dogs. That's why we weed out the ten best as soon as we can and give away the rest.

Now there are not always ten openings to make the team each year, but we gradually have to replenish and rebuild. The youngest dogs that I run in the Kuskokwim 300 are about a year and a half to two years old. The youngest dogs in the Iditarod are two years old. It is like any sports team. You have to blend in rookies with the veterans at the right time so your team doesn't get too old or so it is not inexperienced. Dogs that prove themselves in the Kusko, which is much shorter, of course, are usually the best candidates for the Iditarod team when we need to fill in new members of the team.

Now that Mike Jr. is also racing we have two teams from the kennel entered in the Kusko every year. Junior will have the best team and he will be trying to win. I drive the second team and I want to do the best I can, but the main purpose is to develop young talent for future teams and give those young dogs experience in a racing situation. One team is mainly yearlings and how they perform helps us coaches make the decisions about who makes the "A" team. Actually, sometimes Junior and I flip a coin to see who gets which dogs and he will get mad at me because I get to use a dog he wants.

Over the years I think the best leader we have had is Blackie. Blackie goes back to the 1970s and 1980s. We have had several outstanding leaders in the Iditarod. We always have had. But Blackie was the best of our leaders. He won 99 percent of the races he entered; he was extraordinary. I also once bought a dog from Susan Butcher, a small, red dog, but Blackie is the favorite one.

The pups come from the same few litters, but we have to choose which ones we want in the team. We look for sturdy feet, good fur, and their ability to eat and drink water. The coat is very important because of the cold and they absolutely must be good eaters and drinkers. Dogs burn up thousands of calories a day—some people have estimated it as up to 10,000 calories used—in the Iditarod and they have to restore their energy. You can't have racing dogs that just come into a checkpoint and lie down. They have to want to eat and drink. One thing I look for in a dog is him being hardheaded. What I mean by that is a dog that won't quit. Having good feet is an important characteristic. A dog with sensitive feet can't run a thousand miles.

Now we use booties more along the trail than ever before. In the past we used to only put protective booties on the dogs' feet when the trail was rough. The way the Iditarod has changed is mushers take much longer runs than they used to. If you are going to do hundred-mile runs consistently then you have got to have booties all of the time. That protects the dogs' feet. It's a change in strategy.

Putting together a dog team to race in the Iditarod is not a science. You think you know what you are doing because you have been doing it for a long time, but a lot of dogs will fool you. I have had some dogs that I never thought would make it into the team and they turned out to be very good dogs, some of the best I ever had. When they were running in the Kusko they showed more than I thought that they had in them.

Junior is running the kennel's best dogs in the Iditarod now and it takes sixteen dogs for an Iditarod team. These are the best dogs we ever had, I think, in the current lineup. If we have fifty dogs in the kennel and two teams' worth in training, not all good dogs are going to make the team. I have also had some dogs that I thought were going to be great and they weren't. I remember dropping a dog in Elim that I thought would be one of the best.

Over the years since the start of the Iditarod in the 1970s, the size of racing dogs has gotten smaller. They have been bred that way because they are faster. I like a dog that weighs between fifty and fifty-five pounds, though I have used dogs that weigh in their sixties in recent years. I would rather have a bigger dog that will make it all of the way than a smaller, faster dog that I have to drop. Overall, though, the average person from outside of Alaska, a tourist, who sees an Iditarod team, says, "I thought the dogs would be bigger."

Sometimes I can use the bigger ones because I am a bigger guy, weighing 260 pounds. I think sometimes the dogs that are a little bit bigger are more consistent and have fewer injuries. Whatever size they are Alaska huskies want to run. The animal rights activists who say that we make them run are just wrong. It's in the breed. I like to run, too. I don't mean on foot, but on the sled runners. I like training more than racing, the private experience of going out in the wilderness, the time spent with just me and the dogs sharing. There's not so much pressure, but being out there and setting your own pace about when you want to go and stop is more fun for me.

There are a lot of people who watch the Iditarod who shiver at the sight of snow and ice and when they hear that the temperature might be minus-forty degrees. It is not for everybody. I have a hard time with summers. I do not like summers here. It's miserable with gnats and mosquitoes. I like the weather better from September on. I feel better when it gets cooler. For me, in the early fall, when it is cooling off during moose hunting season, that's the best.

I like the winter when I can get out in the wilderness and do my own thing. I enjoy fishing beneath the ice every day, chipping the ice and getting food for the dogs. It's ongoing work. In the summer we put out fishnets on the Kuskokwim River and traps in the winter. We can also put out nets underneath the ice until Christmastime. I just know that I feel a lot better when I am outside in cold weather. I'd rather be out in the cold with my dogs any time. Traveling out there in the wilderness with the dogs by ourselves gives me a sense of freedom. Yes, I have to deal with the cold and blizzards, but I think that's just part of things, one of the challenges of life. Nobody ever promised life was going to be easy.

The Iditarod was great for me even though I have never come close to winning it and it is so expensive to prepare for and enter. I competed in those three Iditarods and took two years off. After 1997 when I placed eighteenth, I really wanted to continue. I had a few other good races, finishing in the twenties by 2000. I think at that time I liked the challenge of running the Iditarod to see how well I could do. Every race has been different, a new adventure. I spend time with different mushers, different people every year. I just enjoyed being out there and racing straight through 2005 without missing another year.

One year there was no snow in Anchorage, or not enough for dogsleds, or in the Mat-Su Valley, either, and the Iditarod moved the start to Fairbanks. I thought that was an interesting highlight, to start from Fairbanks, and mushing down the Yukon River, but I didn't enjoy the part about trucking the dogs more than 360 miles to Fairbanks. I didn't like that drive with the dogs. The dogs got sick before the race. They weren't used to spending so much time in a truck on the highway. The long drive affected my dogs. We don't have a dog truck in Akiak. I was really worried about them being sick even before we left the starting line. But the move to Fairbanks put a different flavor on the race instead of starting in Anchorage, Wasilla, or Willow, all of the time.

It was something different mushing down the Yukon, going into some different places as checkpoints. I'm glad I got to see some villages like Tanana. I have some friends there and I got to see them. I got to go new places with my dogs.

Of course if you enter the Iditarod you have got to expect the weather to be a factor at some point. Some years it is worse than others. I think the coldest weather I have ever experienced on the Iditarod Trail was in 2005. When I took off from Rainy Pass, the wind was howling and the windchill factor was about a hundred degrees below zero. It was blowing like hell outside of Rainy Pass and the trip through the Dalzell Gorge was one of the hardest, harshest trips I have ever had.

I had to take off my glasses. The condensation from my breathing was fogging my glasses and I took everything off my face and exposed it to the wind or cold for less than a minute. I couldn't see through all of that. We were being hit by winds of seventy or eighty miles per hour, and I think it only took about thirty seconds to freeze my face. My cheeks and nose were frozen when I got to Rohn. That may have been the hardest thing I went through in the Iditarod from a physical standpoint.

I could barely hold on to the sled because the wind was blowing so hard. All of the trail markers were blown down, too. There was no trail. I had a general idea where I was going, but we barely made it into Rohn.

Guessing where I was all of the time was a little dicey. I had been through blizzards on the Bering Sea Coast and those blow holes outside of Nome, but the toughest experience I ever had was between Rainy Pass and the Dalzell Gorge.

I have had frostbite on my fingers from the Iditarod. When you are in the checkpoint and it is minus forty or the wind is making it feel like minus seventy and you take off your gloves to change booties, you run that risk. The weather isn't always that bad. Some years the trail conditions are great and we have perfect weather. I think I was in three races that had perfect weather and the times were very fast to Nome.

Every year I spent time with different mushers on the trail and at checkpoints because of the way the race unfolded. One year I traveled a lot with Sonny King. He was from South Carolina and he had that Southern accent. We took a break at Don's Cabin outside of Ophir and I remember him snoring. I really enjoyed listening to him talk with that accent. After we took a nap at the cabin and we woke up I said, "Hey, Sonny King! You have that Southern accent and you snored so hard you even snored Southern."

At first I was surprised to hear that there was a musher from South Carolina in the race. But Sonny was a veterinarian and he had been around the block a few times. He started to race with dogs that belonged to Doug Swingley, the four-time champion. I really enjoyed being around Sonny. We spent a lot of time together that year. He's a pretty tough guy.

One race I spent a lot of time running with Zack Steer. He is a very fine young man and after watching him race I told him, "Zack, you're going to win this race one of these years. Do your best. I know with your dog care and your attitude being positive all of the time you will do well in the Iditarod and some time you are going to win it."

He is from a family of athletes. One of his sisters, Rachel, was on the US Olympic biathlon team. His other sister, Becky, was a triathlon competitor. Sure enough Zack did finish third in the 2007 race. But recently he gave up racing, at least for now, to spend more time with his family, I believe. But after traveling with him I felt he could win the Iditarod. For now his kids come first and that is a good priority.

I was glad that the Iditarod started paying prize money for the top thirty finishers instead of the top twenty because the competition gets harder and harder. There are so many good teams out there now. These are the best mushers in the world. Guys like Bill Cotter, Zack Steer, Joe Garnie, Rick Swenson, Paul Gephardt, DeeDee Jonrowe, Doug Swingley, Jeff King, Martin Buser, the Seaveys, they are the best in the world at what they do and only one team can win each year. It's really hard. Some very good mushers retired without winning the Iditarod, but they had very good careers.

CHAPTER 15

A big difference since I first started racing in the Iditarod to now is that the pace of the race has gotten faster and faster. I would finish as high as eighteenth and then all of a sudden I was finishing much lower. There are more good, competitive mushers than ever, but I got faster, too.

One guy I marveled at watching him in the checkpoints was Hans Gatt. I think he is finally retired, although he said he was retired before and came back. He won the Yukon Quest more than once. He was so efficient and he had good dogs.

I was traveling with him one time and looking at his team and I teased him by hollering, "Hans! Gatt damn, you've got good dogs!" He was a good driver and just a very efficient guy to watch perform his tasks.

In 1989 I finished the Iditarod in twenty-third for the second time in a row. I did a lot of traveling with Sonny King and Sonny Lindner. For a while there, I was between the Sonnys. Later, I traveled with Tim Osmar and Joe Garnie most of the time. Tim is good company, but Joe Garnie is the best. Sonny Lindner always had a smile on his face and he is a good guy on the trail. He won the first Yukon Quest in 1984 and he is still going. He had some of his best races recently when he was in his sixties.

Although the race has gotten much faster I don't think the dogs have gotten much faster. I think they are running longer and resting less. The race used to be won in fourteen days, then twelve, eleven, ten, and when it got to nine nobody thought it would ever get into the eight-day area, but it did. Still, the dogs are not running faster, but the training, the equipment, and nutrition programs have allowed the dogs to run much longer at one time without taking such long rests. They can keep up the pace.

The dogs can maintain a fast pace and the mushers are going much longer without sleep. I don't know how they can do it without sleeping more. I say the dogs will never break down, but the human being will. That's how tough the dogs are. The humans will break down. The fatigue will get the human to slow down or maybe quit when the dogs won't.

Even though these are the best dog mushers in the world they can't keep up with the dogs, on foot when they are running, and for overall stamina.

As long as you take care of the dogs, rest them properly, hydrate them, feed them, they will never break down just from running hard. I think the driver is the weakest link. Sometimes the driver fails to eat properly, drink enough water, and he makes bad judgments because of that. If the dogs refuse to go it is because the human has not fed or watered them enough. The dogs will just sit down and not move. You cannot make a dog run. It's the musher.

In 2000, I finished the Iditarod in 10 days, 19 hours, 21 minutes. That was a fast race for me, but I finished twenty-eighth. I spent a lot of time racing with David Sawatzky and Aaron Burmeister. Sonny King did well that year. That was his best race. A lot of us were very close together in that same ten-day range. A few hours here and a few hours there, we were a fairly tight group. That was a fast trail and we had good weather all of the way.

During the 2001 race my dogs got sick on the trail and I finished thirty-seventh. I was still feeling pretty strong myself, too. I felt good. It gets a little bit harder athletically as you get past fifty and then sixty. You can start to feel the difference on your body. I dropped off a little bit that year. I think the conditions were tougher. At fifty, I didn't feel much different, but when I got past fifty-five years old I started feeling my age a little bit. You are tired and stiff. They are long days on the trail and it is pretty hard to recover.

Every time I did the Iditarod between 1992 and 2000 I kept gathering the sobriety pledges and carrying the signatures in my sled to Nome. It was an effort. It took a lot of time and it took more time as I went on. There were a lot of people volunteering to gather them, but it still took a lot of effort from me. Overall, during that time period, I believe I carried 400,000 signatures along the trail.

After the 2000 race I couldn't afford my time anymore. With the level of volunteers we had I just couldn't maintain it because it kept growing. Some people think I still do it. It was an institutionalized thing. I put a lot of time into it because I was very concerned about the condition of our people. I have either seen or lived through the bad conditions caused by alcohol. I think it was all worth the effort and it made an impact on some policies in villages. It has led to the type of leadership we are seeing on the alcohol issue in the tribes.

There is a lot of work that still needs to be done in the tribes internally and initiatives need to be taken by each village across Alaska on its own. The ideas are there for healthy communities and wellness and the efforts to reclaim our lands, reclaim our culture, and reclaim our language. We need to restore things that have broken down. We need to fix those things. Hopefully, with the signatures I planted a seed in each of those individuals approached and who signed pledges to make the choice on their own to give up alcohol for a year. It was like a contract between me and them. But it was up to them to live up to that contract. I think many of them tried and many of them changed. You always wonder about those individuals, the 400,000 individuals, and whether or not they made a permanent change.

It's really impossible to know how many succeeded given the numbers. If fifty percent of them succeeded that would be 200,000 people getting sober. To be safe, I would guess ten percent got sober and stayed that way. That would be 40,000 people. So it's worth the effort we put into it and in some people's minds when they see me that's what they think of me doing.

Actually, in the 2002 race I had some problems on the trail. I crashed between Happy River and Rainy Pass and I was knocked out. The sled hit a tree and I hit my head on the tree. Bam! I was lying on the ground—I don't know how long—and then somebody was waking me up. It was Martin Buser and he was going, "Are you OK? Are you OK? What happened?" I said, "I hit a tree." He got me up and helped me take the sled out of the jam in the trees. I knew my head wasn't straight after the crash so I took my time from there. I had never had anything like that happen to me before on the trail. I ended up helping Melanie Gould. All of the females in her team were in heat and she was having a tough time controlling them. She was leading me and I would catch up. Those dogs were in heat for hundreds of miles. I never did go to the doctor about my head. I probably had a concussion. Maybe that's why I'm crazy.

I kept going after I hit my head, but I didn't care about competing anymore during that race. I took my time to get to Nome. It's a good thing Martin woke me up.

One of my challenges along the Iditarod Trail when I was trying to race was how much time I spent in the village checkpoints talking to people. I did want to talk to everyone, but it slowed me down some. I did move up seven places to finish thirty-first in 2003. I was with Melanie Gould on the trail again and Jessie Royer, Lynda Plettner, and Robert Bundtzen. It seems I am always hanging around with Robert. He is a good guy. The people I see the most on the trail are Robert and Cindy Gallea. It just seems to work out that way with our dogs.

In 2004, I finished in thirty-seventh place. I had a pretty decent team and I thought I could do better, but I didn't feel like pushing the dogs hard a lot. I kind of held back and just rode. If the musher was a more hard-core guy I might have finished higher. I was with Robert Bundtzen and Lynda Plettner again.

Leading up to the 2005 Iditarod finances were an issue again. I wasn't sure I was going to be able to race, although I wanted to do it. There were some problems. I had to work full-time and doing the training too was tough. I had some family help in order to make it to the starting line. Mike Jr. was coming around and Shawna helped. The kids got involved more with the feeding and the training and the mushing became more of a family endeavor. I finished thirty-sixth that year.

If you are working from nine A.M. to five P.M. somebody has to pick up the slack in the dog yard and the kids did. I would get home and work with the dogs and train after five P.M. until eight or nine o'clock most days and some days not until midnight. I was working full-time and trying to do all of that.

In 2006, I could not even race. I could not afford it. It was about finances again. I signed up, but I didn't have any cash, so I withdrew. I looked at it as a time-out and hoped I would be able to come back. I didn't look at it as retirement. I looked over the lay of the land before I had to fly the team to Anchorage and I said, "I can't afford to." There was nobody in my family to help me financially.

Finances are always going to be a bigger deal if you live in rural Alaska than if you are a musher who lives on the road system. It's a lot cheaper to do the feeding. It costs between $14 and $19 to ship a forty-pound bag of food from Anchorage. The cost of living in Akiak is triple what it is in Anchorage, I think. The biggest factor is transportation costs, flying everything in.

I have a truck in Akiak. I bought it in Anchorage and shipped it to Bethel on an air cargo plane. In the winter I drove it from Bethel to Akiak on the ice road on the Kuskokwim River. That's how you get a vehicle here. After you buy the vehicle the shipping cost from Anchorage to Bethel is between $4,000 and $7,000. It seems to be harder to get sponsors if you live in the Bush, too. GCI, the communications company, was a pretty consistent sponsor for me up until a couple of years ago. I have written to Native corporations over the years and they did not sponsor me until recent times. My little village corporation put in some money. The tribe put in $500 or $1,000. One year I had help from Northern Air Cargo shipping the dogs between Bethel and Anchorage and from Nome to Bethel. I have had some pockets of sponsorship that helped ease the pain of expenses, but they were not consistent. And many of the sponsors were small.

No one enters the Iditarod with the belief that they are going to get rich. Nope. That doesn't happen. I wanted to break even every time I entered, but it was never the case. I always ended up having to pay bills for transportation. I had to work full-time and train full-time. In 2007 I finished in thirty-ninth place and in 2008 I did not race again for money reasons.

In 2009 I spent more time working than training and I didn't have enough miles on the team to be competitive. That year I did not carry sobriety pledges in my sled, but I did something else to honor a person who died because someone else took drugs and drank alcohol. Dr. Roger Gollub, who was a pediatrician in Anchorage, had gotten into mushing the previous November, but he was killed by a drunk driver on a snow-machine outside of Kotzebue. I carried his obituary from the newspaper, a love letter, a family photograph, and a stethoscope in the sled to honor his memory. Later, the guy who hit him with the snowmachine received a long prison term.

I had a big struggle just to finish the race. I really did. It was a challenge, but I did not think I was going to retire from the Iditarod. But in 2010 Mike Jr. was ready to race. It was his turn after helping me so much. He had been running in the Kuskokwim 300 for a while. He didn't say much, but I think he always had an interest in running the Iditarod, so he worked to make sure he was eligible for the 2010 race. He ran his qualifying races and he was prepared to run his first Iditarod. We thought about having two teams, but we could never afford that.

With having only one team in the Iditarod we didn't have to split up the best dogs the way we did in the Kusko. Mike got to pick from all of the best dogs in the kennel. It made a lot of sense for the family, too. I had to work and he was mushing better than I was. I stepped back and let him race the Iditarod.

CHAPTER 16

In 2010 the Mike Williams in the Iditarod became Mike Jr. He had been racing in the Kuskokwim 300 and between 2009 and 2010 Junior got himself qualified for the Iditarod by competing in shorter races. Besides the Kusko, he also ran the Kobuk 440. He was ready to run the Iditarod. We had talked about it for a couple of years, but there was no way we could afford to enter two teams.

That year I wanted to give him the chance to fulfill his dream of running the Iditarod. He had always had it in the back of his mind. He had earned his chance with his racing and by helping me out in the kennel when I needed it over the years.

After two times in the Kusko where I beat him, he began to slow down and take care of the dogs and conserve their energy. He learned from his mistakes. Once he went into a ditch with the dogs and the sled and I had to pull him out. Mike showed he was ready for the Iditarod in the 2009 Kusko when he almost won that race. I felt good about how he did against all of the top mushers that were in the race and so I felt good about him going to the starting line for the Iditarod.

My thinking was that Mike would just have a good race and finish the Iditarod as a rookie. He finished twenty-sixth. I thought he would do pretty well and my expectation for him was just that he finish, take good care of himself, and take good care of the dogs. From there he would do the best he could and finish where he could. He finished in the money as a rookie and I felt he was beginning to establish himself. He sniffed out the trail, got a taste of the conditions, and was finding out about himself as a musher out there.

When Mike finished, I said, "Congratulations. You did a good job." I was in Nome to watch him finish and he looked really good when he came in and crossed under the arch on Front Street. He didn't seem to be beat up like I was. He was twenty-five and I was thirty-seven when I started. I was almost over the hill already. I should have started running the Iditarod at age twenty-five.

For a rookie Mike did a really good job and since we could not afford to send two teams on the trail I let him pretty much take over for a while. I didn't tell people that I was retired, but I stepped back. I did not run in 2010, 2011, or 2012. The game plan for the family had changed. Instead of helping me get ready to do the Iditarod, I helped him get ready to do the Iditarod. I became a little bit of a coach and made recommendations to him since I knew a lot of the tales of the trail. For whatever worth they had for him, I told him things.

Some things were more important than others. I told him to start out slow, not go out too fast, and rest the dogs carefully. I suggested that he rest them a lot in the beginning and then start picking up the pace when they got to the Yukon River. I told him to just mush his own pace and look after the dogs and determine what their own pace was. Just do what they tell you they can do. I wanted him to have a good time in his first Iditarod and I was very happy with his twenty-sixth-place finish.

The next year he raced like a veteran. Mike finished in thirteenth place and his time was very fast at 9 days, 11 hours, 59 minutes. We had a good year of training and we did enter two teams in the Kusko, so that helped him come up with the best sixteen dogs from the kennel. He trained hard and I helped him. He thinks things through and he tends to details more than I do. I just focus on the big picture, but he's a detail man. He watches the dogs' performance and what he can get out of the dogs. He had been racing around Akiak and Bethel for a long time and winning a lot of the races. So he had quite a bit of race experience locally. Mike won the 150-miler as part of the Kusko and that trophy is in our living room. He took to mushing early and he worked hard to get better. In that 150-miler he blew them away and beat everybody by a half hour.

Mike's second race was very good. That was pretty good speed. Again I was very happy with his finish. It was only his second long race of a thousand miles. Him and his friend Pete Kaiser—they grew up together and competed with the family kennels and Pete started in the Iditarod the same year as Mike and is also doing very well. Pete's father Ron and my brother Walter were competitors in the earlier days. Our best leader was Blackie and Ron's best leader was Whitey. So you had Blackie and Whitey competing, but Blackie won more races than Whitey did.

Pete Kaiser was right there, too, in Mike's second Iditarod, finishing eighth. They were two young guys making a mark at the same time and kind of announcing themselves to the mushing world that they were going to be there. There are other young ones taking over in the Iditarod now, too. Dallas Seavey has already won twice. Mike and Pete Kaiser will have their own opportunities. I'm with the group that is getting old and they are with the group that can take over. I think they have a shot to win it. But some of the older guys are still around. Sonny Lindner is one tough "kid." He's my Elder.

We will continue to do the best we can with the dogs. Both of us will keep doing the Kusko and using that to form a team for the Iditarod. Mike has been right there with the best mushers at the end and he has recorded the fastest time from Safety to Nome over the last twenty-two miles. He has finished right with John Baker, Mitch Seavey, and DeeDee Jonrowe. He's doing a good job for a young guy and he has a lot of potential.

Leading up to the 2013 race Mike asked me if I was going to enter. I finally said, "Yeah, I'm gonna go." I decided to sign up so I could run the Iditarod once at the same time as my son. It is probably the only time we will do it together. Part of the reason is that I am getting older and part of the reason is that we don't have the money to enter two teams in one year unless circumstances change. Junior is now the primary racer in the family. He will do better in the race than I will. So it was basically going to be a one-time thing.

It was a special thing to be out there with my son except that he wasn't racing that fast. We were traveling together between Anchorage and Nikolai and I finally told him, "Get the hell out of my sight." I didn't want him to stay behind with me. I told him, "Quit hanging around me." I knew he had better dogs. After Nikolai he disappeared. I told him I could take care of myself. But it was great to see him out there and once in a lifetime for us to have a father and son out there. There have been others who have done it, of course. Mitch Seavey and Dallas, Joe Redington and Raymie. The Barrons. In 2013, it was the Williamses' chance for both of us to go. I'm glad I did, though it was logistically tough and expensive to put two teams in.

The transportation was very expensive. The preparation took a lot of time. I tried not to worry too much about getting the food drops ready and all of the preparations, but I expended a lot of time. I took care of getting the food to Anchorage because I wanted Mike to keep training the dogs. I did the bagging and getting equipment ready. I wanted him to get the dogs sharp. After Mike left me behind in Nikolai I never saw him on the trail again until we were both at the finish line in Nome. He finished twenty-third and I finished forty-fifth.

I told him I was glad to see him there and again congratulations. I was glad I made it to Nome and accomplished the goal of finishing in the same race as my son. If it was the only time and opportunity we had to do it together I was glad we had the chance. It may never happen again for us, though I am not going to say that I am retired from the Iditarod, only that I am on intermission. Junior is taking over for now. We can only afford to run one team and he is going to be the driver. We will try to finish in a way that is a good finish, the best we can do. That's the goal.

One thing I worry about is how many Alaska Natives keep entering the Iditarod—or do not. It is a reflection of how much money it costs to run the Iditarod, especially if you live in rural Alaska. I think there was one race back there when I was the only Eskimo Native in it. In the older days we had guys like Emmitt Peters and Joe Garnie all of the time. There was a lean period when there was practically no one from the Bush. That was hard to see and I hope it never becomes a case where nobody can afford to go. Things are a little better now and it was a great thing when John Baker won the race in 2011.

There was a time when I was almost the only one. I got e-mails just to say to me, "I'm glad you are doing this or it would be an embarrassment." I am not sure how it happened where so many people went away. Money was probably a big thing. Age was a factor for some. Some mushers retired and there was no replacement. It should never happen that there are only one or two Alaska Natives in the race. There should be an increase, not a decrease. Maybe Native corporations can help more. At one time I thought of organizing a sponsor pool for the Iditarod and it would be geared to funding races for Alaska Natives. The pool would raise money and distribute it, cut checks, to help out with entry fees, dog food, and transportation.

There are some young, talented mushers who could do it. There are some mushers who only race in the 150-miler at the Kusko and that's all they can afford because they don't have large kennels. They just can't afford to feed as many dogs as it takes to put together a high-caliber Iditarod team. You must have a decent-sized kennel in order to find the right quality of dogs to fill out a team. You can't run the Iditarod when you have just sixteen dogs in your yard and expect all sixteen to be good ones. The absolute minimum, I believe, is to have thirty dogs and that's a small kennel. Once you have the thirty you still have to train about twenty-four of them. From there you would choose the best sixteen for the Iditarod. And it costs a lot of money to feed them and time to train them that you can't be using for a regular office job.

I think we have usually had about fifty dogs. Some of them are puppies and yearlings. We pick out the top twenty-four and prepare them. Twenty-four athletes, not young ones or old ones, twenty-four runnable dogs. If we are going to enter two teams in the Iditarod then we have to have about forty runnable dogs. If you take out the geriatrics and the young ones, that's just about all we have. We have to train that many and make sure they have race toughness built into them.

My daughter Shawna has thought about racing, but she became a teacher. She spends some time training the dogs and feeding them and she has done some local races. I would certainly be comfortable in having her run the Kusko sometime and I think she would do well. She's really good with the dogs and knows what to do and how to take care of dogs. Maybe sometime after she is established as a teacher she will do some races. But she has kids, a family, and bills.

Where we live a big part of what we feed the dogs is salmon, fish that come from the Kuskokwim River in our nets. We eat the fish and the dogs eat the fish. Fishing to us is living. It is life. Without fish we're hungry. We're dead. The people and the dogs in Akiak, in lots of places in rural Alaska, just don't have any way of living without fish. We catch it and preserve it for the winter. We catch it and feed it to the dogs the same day. If you don't do that here you go to the welfare office and get public assistance. Some people just try to live off of the cans we have on the shelves in our small grocery store. I think that's very unhealthy. I'd rather eat fish and live off the fish. That's what we live on and depend on.

I know a lot of mushers who live on the road system and they feed their dogs the high-nutrient, manufactured dog food that comes in bags. I know it is good for the dogs, but I think the fish is good for the dogs, too, and we can't afford to ship in all of that food. King salmon, Chinook, is the best. Then there are red salmon and chum salmon. Chums are really good. We dry and can salmon for ourselves. We take fresh fish out of the river and cook it up in barrels for the dogs when they are caught. Those are our extra-large outdoor cookstoves.

Cooking up fish for the dogs is part of our daily routine. When I was traveling Mike Jr. did the work and fed them. Now we all help Mike. If he is around he is in the dog yard every day, but the family helps feed the dogs that run in the Iditarod. We all share a part in it even if he is the main musher now.

In the early days of the Iditarod just about everyone fed their dogs fish. Nobody knew how many calories they needed to run a thousand miles and it was only as the breed developed and the food manufacturers developed a higher grade of food that was suitable for long-distance running dogs that so many other people changed what they did.

It's nice if you have a dog food sponsor, but not all of us do. And we live right here next to a river that produces the best fish in the world, so we take advantage of that. Having dogs and fishing are two of the most important aspects of our lives and feeding fish we catch to the dogs is where the two things overlap.

The dogs seem to like the fish almost as much as I do.

CHAPTER 17

It is impossible to overestimate the amount of importance that fishing and fish from the Kuskokwim River have in our lives. There is fishing with set nets, canning, drying, salting, and preserving fish for the rest of the year. We do some kind of fishing about ten months of the year. The other two months the river is frozen up, though some of that frozen time offers opportunities for ice fishing.

A lot of the dried fish we prepare goes into the freezer for the winter. We're saving for those two months where we can't catch any fish. It feels like we're always fishing. This is all with nets. I do not own a rod and reel that people use for sport-fishing. This is subsistence fishing to the feed the family.

In the area next to our land where we have our boat the river is between eight and fifteen feet in depth. The mesh set net, which is strung out in the river, is about fifty feet long. The salmon or other fish are swimming along in the river and they get tangled in the mesh under the water. Once or twice a day we come out and pick the fish out of the net. The net is in the migratory path of the fish. There's a small eddy there where we place the net. We always look for the best spots where the fish will come through. We only need one net.

We can drift in the boat—the boat is aluminum with a flat bottom and is eighteen feet long—with the net out. On a good drift we might get a hundred to two hundred fish. When the fish are really running we might get that many fish in just a ten-minute drift. Other times if the fish aren't running you can come out and check the net and there might be only five fish. Just yesterday we hauled in ten fish and that wasn't a particularly good catch for twenty-four hours. I think the net got tangled up and it was riding too low in the water. Fish swam over it. The main reason I use the boat is for set-net fishing. We can cross the river to the opposite shore.

We feed the dogs in the morning and it is usually soup. Then we give them snacks and that is cooked fish. We pick the fish out of the nets and sometimes just throw it into the barrel that we use as the cooker. It's different in the winter. I use a propane cooker and put some kibble in the mix, commercial dog food, and some extra vitamin supplements. I also give the dogs plenty of water, maybe three or four cups every morning. When we're running the dogs we also give them snacks along the way. They get dinner at the end of the day, too. Every day they get a bowl of soup with fish or meat in it. Sometimes it is birds or beaver meat, whatever we can get. Mostly that is game food, not commercial dog food.

There are hours invested every day in feeding the dogs in the morning and evening. Every single day. In the summer, when the dogs aren't training and working hard they live mostly on salmon. Salmon and whitefish make up the main food in the summer. They only need a couple thousand calories a day because they are lying around a lot not doing much. It is when they are training that they might need 5,000 or more calories a day and while competing in the Iditarod it can be up to 10,000 calories.

After the Iditarod in March the dogs get a chance to rest. Sometimes we start training as early as July, more often in August or September. If it is particularly hot in the summer—for here that means it may be seventy or so—we might wait a little longer than usual. This is very basic, light training. We might hook up ten dogs to a four-wheeler and run them three times a week for two to four miles or sometimes six miles. It's just fine-tuning, a little bit of conditioning, not really race training. It's background. They are easing back into training. The four-wheeler enables them to run over dirt trails.

It's always a fun time with the dogs. Shawna is usually here helping. Junior is there. My son-in-law Gilbert helps out. The grandkids are around. Everybody gets in on it and we try to have three short runs a day for the dogs. It could be twelve dogs at a time or fourteen. Getting out on the four-wheeler is just stretching out, toughening them up. It's not the real thing. We just go around town so it is hard to do more than four or five miles at a time since town is so small. It's always more fun on snow. It pretty much doesn't snow enough to go out until October.

I wish the snow would come earlier, in September, like it has in the past. We always had snow in September, maybe mid-September when I was a kid. Now it's near the end of October, about a month later. The first snow doesn't necessarily stay, either. It takes until November to have snow on the ground for the season. Everything seems a month later than it used to be. Climate change and global warming are happening. There are naysayers, but they need some education and common-sense training. There is global warming and we can tell here in Akiak. There is still some denial, but there needs to be some wake-up call.

We are seeing such extreme weather all over and I am sure that comes from global warming. Hurricane Sandy and Hurricane Katrina, tornadoes in the Midwest, snow on the East Coast, flooding. There is still denial. I don't think the politicians are listening, or hearing. I look at the political process and I shake my head and I *am* a politician of a sort.

I have been in politics in some way for a long time. I was the student body president in high school. I got involved with the Akiak Native Community Tribal Council forty years ago, and the village corporation board. It is called the Kokarmuit Corporation. When I came back from Bethel I immediately started working on it. I kind of got drafted to be involved, but I have stayed involved.

One of the first big issues in front of us, and this is a big issue everywhere, of course, was the education of our kids. We wanted our kids to be educated in Akiak and not have to go elsewhere for high school like I did. We were able to erect a high school here because of the Molly Hootch case, but we also wanted to take control of the curriculum.

We wanted to get community involvement in the education of our children from kindergarten on. We had never been involved since the government came in and the Bureau of Indian Affairs ran things. That was something that was important to me and that was one issue that pushed me to be involved in tribal matters and on other boards. We wanted to have our say in our own community and that included the hiring and firing of teachers. We had never been involved. The teachers were hired by the BIA and that was all under the policy of assimilation.

Once the Indian Self-Determination and Education Assistance Act of 1975 passed we approached the BIA and told them we wanted to take over the education of our children. We wanted to be involved in shaping our kids' education and in keeping our kids here in town. They said no, they didn't think we could do it because we had never managed the children's education before. We answered back to the BIA that yes we could provide the education. The tribal council passed a resolution saying we had every right to do so under that law. The BIA said no, but the law said yes and we wanted to do it. We passed a resolution to contract for education with the BIA and forced them to pay for it while we managed the educational system. That was what the act of 1975 provided for. It took five years of negotiations to get it going. In 1980 we had a signed agreement that we would take the contract dollars from the Bureau of Indian Affairs and hire our own teachers and develop our own curriculum. We began managing the program and it was funded by the BIA. That was the first ever contract through the BIA with an Alaska tribe. Others followed. Once other communities heard about the deal we made they wanted to do the same thing. So we set the precedent.

It all began with K through eight, but the long-term goal was to get a high school going in Akiak. The Molly Hootch case was settled before our negotiations were finally concluded, so that led to the building of the high school. The education of our children was a trust obligation from the federal government. When the state gave in on the Molly Hootch case, it became the state's responsibility to build high schools in each community. That meant no more splitting up families and forcing kids to attend boarding schools a thousand miles away if they wanted to continue their education.

For a while there was a tribal school and a BIA school operating. There was a sense of competition in a small community. It was a parental choice. We managed the tribal school for five years and we got better at hiring and shaping a culturally relevant curriculum. That included using our own language. We burned those "Dick and Jane" books and they were replaced by culturally relevant stories.

Those books were developed by the University of Alaska in Bethel and the characters had Yup'ik faces. The kids had a Yup'ik mom and dad. We had a bonfire burning books that were foreign to our culture that were being imposed on our kids. They represented cultural genocide for our people.

In 1985, US Senator Ted Stevens got the funding for our tribal school cut off through a congressional act. He said the state of Alaska had the obligation to educate each child and that the federal government was running out of money. We objected to that because we believe the federal government has the obligation to educate each tribal child. Senator Stevens got those funds sliced off. But then he was able to raise funding in order to have the Bureau of Indian Affairs schools comply with state standards with fire escapes and water. Senator Stevens got our funding cut because we were not assimilating and we were providing top-notch education to our children in our own way. We wanted to make sure they did not lose their identity, their language, or their culture. We were empowering parents to be involved in educating their children. But there were two schools and I think money became an issue. It seemed like a duplication of services.

Now the state has its own standards and state-operated schools and they are shaped by the Department of Education. We have an advisory school board. It would have been interesting to see what would have happened if Alaska had not had all of the oil money it did when the Molly Hootch decision came down. I don't know how they would have afforded to build these schools. All of this is besides our belief—where we were in disagreement with Senator Stevens—that the federal government had the obligation to provide educational services to tribes, and health care, too. If

Alaska did not have the oil money I don't see how it would have been possible for the state to follow up on what was agreed to with the court and build new schools in villages. We spent five years developing and instituting our own educational operation. It was progressive and we were on the verge of solidifying our curriculum under the control of Akiak. Then that was cut and the services were taken over by the Regional Educational Attendance Area law.

We disbanded our attempts when the money got cut off. Then we approached the state to try to form our own school district. We asked the state legislature to allow us to secede from the Lower Kuskokwim School District. We had a public referendum in 1985 that passed and we formed a Yupiit School District that consisted of Akiak, Tuluksak, and Akiachak. Chevak voted to become its own single site school district. It passed by only one vote in Akiak. We lost the federal money because Senator Stevens took it away on a rider to a bill. Now our funding comes from the state. But we were able to form our own school board and hire our own superintendent.

It was satisfying that we got our own high school in town. We had been forced to raise our children the best we could with them going away to boarding school. I had to go away for high school, but my kids went to high school in Akiak. And they were able to stay home with the family. I think a lot of harm was done to families before, but that's done with. Right now Molly Hootch is enjoyed by each community, but we have still been deprived as tribes from the obligation of the federal government and we were deprived of lands.

That was a huge deal. We were able to hire and fire our own teachers and help shape the curriculum while meeting the state requirements. We could still keep the curriculum culturally relevant. I think the best education is provided when parents have a say. They never had that say before. In 1985, I was elected to serve on our regional school board from the get-go. We hired our superintendents and we fired some, too. We took care of business as we saw fit. If we had a good school leader we kept him. If we thought the leader was bad we fired him. But we had never enjoyed that privilege before. I believe I served on the Association of Alaska School Boards from 1988 to 1994. It was a six-year term with term limits.

There were fifty-three school districts in the state and the association was in position to shape state policy on education in rural areas, the REAAs. We shaped these resolutions about culturally relevant curriculums in the Yupitt School District and submitted them to the Association of Alaska School Boards for consideration. When I was sent to the board the first resolution I presented was to ban alcohol from Association of Alaska School Boards functions. It passed unanimously and right away. Before that the association did serve alcohol at its functions.

We were able to advocate for culturally relevant programs in each of the school districts, but the association did not order it. The districts were told they could shape their own culturally relevant program. The school boards still had the power to make those decisions at the local level.

We required the teaching of Alaska history and Alaska's history through the eyes of its Native people. We felt each child should know those things. I helped get those things passed.

There is also much more knowledge and understanding of Native games because of the World Eskimo-Indian Olympics in Fairbanks each summer and through the Native Youth Olympics. The Johnson-O'Malley Indian Education Programs are basically funded for cultural activities, but that portion of Alaska Native money was not cut by Senator Stevens. The University of Alaska has a teaching placement program and they provide teacher preparation for teachers who are going to stay in the state. They have to meet requirements for their licenses that show they have had cultural teaching and sensitivity.

A lot of teachers come to rural Alaska and only stay for one year. They want to see what it is like and try it once, just like entering the Iditarod. Sometimes they spend a year and realize that being in a small village that is more than ninety percent Native and is off the road system isn't for them. That frequently happens with teachers that come from Outside. They are curious about Alaska, but they are not prepared for Akiak culturally or the winter weather. It is a long winter, but they are less prepared for the culture, the language, and the way of life.

Akiak is a small community. There are no operas or baseball games to go to and no shopping malls. They know all of that before they come, but they miss it. One thing we offered to new teachers was a six-hundred level course about our culture and language. We provided this graduate course free of charge. We thought it might help prevent them from burning out. We came up with that because of all the turnover we had with teachers. The turnover is pretty bad. It's about sixty percent every year.

There are about ten or twelve teachers from Outside working in Akiak at a given time. Housing is provided for them. They're supported. We try to do everything we can to support the teachers so they can last here for quite some time. But it is still difficult. They come from California, New York, Indiana, from everywhere. Sometimes it is not so hard to determine which teachers are going to make it in Akiak and which ones are not. I think the teachers that last are educated in their understanding of our world. They understand how we live and the condition of our communities. They recognize that we do certain different things in our culture than in their culture. That might be fishing and hunting and the language. The ways of doing things here are a little different from in the average nuclear white family.

I also served on the state board of education for eight years, between 1994 and 2002. What we did while I was on the board was to start a partnership with the regions to try to develop teachers in rural Alaska because the turnover was so large everywhere. We wanted to develop homegrown teachers. We came up with a rural educators prep program and we funded some REAAs with that money to encourage hiring local teacher aides to take college courses and become certified teachers. My wife, Maggie, was one of the people who took advantage of that. She started as a teacher's aide and obtained her teaching certificate and teaches kindergarten.

Maggie was a teacher's aide before through a rural education preparatory program. She took courses and got certified. We started this because we thought about who would be best to teach our children. We decided it was our own people. That would get rid of the problem of teacher turnover and the problem of communication. The teachers would understand the culture and shouldn't experience cabin fever and leave.

So far in Akiak we were successful in getting two of our teacher aides out of ten certified. Maggie is one of them. The other teacher aides had additional obligations because of family and things like that and they couldn't do it. It took four years for Maggie and Alberta, our next-door neighbor, to become certified. The Yupitt School District now has its own website to advertise for teachers and before that we were mainly using the teacher placement program out of the University of Alaska Fairbanks. There were also job fairs in the spring in Anchorage every year. All of the school districts go there. I would go as a school board member and advertise our school district. We were introducing ourselves.

I would say that Akiak was a good place for you and we need you to teach our children. I explained what type of students we had and gave them all of the information about salary and retirement benefits. I've been involved in doing that for twenty-five years. There are other job fairs in Seattle, Montana, and California, but we mainly use programs inside Alaska.

Over the years I have been involved in interviewing candidates along with an administrator while we're searching for prospective teachers and I have learned that the first impression is probably the right one. That person won't make it in Akiak or that person can make it in Akiak. We had a list of twenty questions that we asked everyone, things like asking if they had any experience in teaching in rural Alaska and how much knowledge they had of various cultures in Alaska. Some of the people applying had never set foot in Alaska. We ask the teacher candidates about how much they know of our climate and weather. Are they able to withstand a temperature of minus fifty degrees and high winds?

We asked what they knew about the Yup'ik people, what their experience was in working with people from cultures other than their own, and whether they've ever dealt with students speaking other languages. I don't think it will ever happen that we get a speaker of our language from someone who is from Outside. All of my kids are bilingual. Maggie and I made sure they knew the Yup'ik language as a first language. Some of the younger kids are losing it pretty fast. It is rapid.

Some young people have married Spanish-speaking people and others from Outside and they move back and their kids cannot understand Yup'ik. Some of them speak broken English. The majority of little kids cannot understand Yup'ik. That's pretty sad. We're trying to provide immersion programs. Maggie did that for a little while, but that burnt her out because there wasn't enough immersion material in the school.

We were trying to teach Yup'ik immersion in elementary school, but then the No Child Left Behind Act came around through President George W. Bush. This is not Texas. They had all of those rules with standardized tests and it worked against us. We had to scale back on the immersion to fifty-fifty. Yup'ik is still taught, but it was cut down dramatically because we had to meet the other standards. Under the law you need to produce those test results or the state can take over your education program.

If there are about 350 people in Akiak maybe 250 of them speak Yup'ik. I would say it's around eighty percent. The majority of people my age speak it, but the younger ones don't. I believe that in the course of my lifetime we might be on the verge of being a dying language. I don't think it will be extinct, but it's vulnerable. I think it could happen if we don't revive it. There are some language studies from the University of Alaska that look at these things and they are supposed to be following if a language is in danger.

I looked on the Internet and found something that said there are 21,000 Central Alaska Yup'iks and that 13,000 of them speak the language. There is a relationship to Central Siberian Yupiks and Alaska Peninsula Yup'iks, and Pacific Yup'iks. We understand each other, but I am very concerned. I am not surprised to see that it is as small a number of speakers as they say. I think combining the Alaska areas it is 15,000 speakers. If we don't work on it now it's going to be rapidly disappearing because of the older people dying. The opportunity to do something is in the school, but it is not the top priority there.

Money always comes up as a reason why things don't happen in the schools. Around 2004 a lawsuit was filed called Moore vs. State of Alaska. It was filed by a parent in Wasilla against Alaska, saying that the state neglected school funding to regional school districts in rural Alaska. I was part of that lawsuit. The group called Citizens for the Educational Advancement of Alaska's Children was the organization that pushed it. We claimed the state had paid out only sixty cents on the dollar of what it should have paid since statehood. The court said that the state had spent enough money and set appropriate standards, but not to the lowest level school districts. In 2012, a settlement was made. The state ended up paying $18 million to the poorest performing school districts. To me that was only a drop in the bucket, or not even that much.

CHAPTER 18

One of the saddest things affecting Natives in Alaska is how many young men end up in jail. They drink too much alcohol and it gets them into trouble. They take drugs and that gets them into trouble. Part of this is high unemployment in the villages. They do not see a future for themselves. They cannot get a good paying job and they despair.

In Akiak we instituted a Therapeutic Court. It is like a drug board. Instead of a traditional court where people get sent to prison for taking drugs we have a treatment program for offenders and those criminals go through an appropriate treatment program. In this program they're not just punished, but they are treated in a way that they can overcome their low self-esteem and their addictions.

The idea is to reduce recidivism. Hopefully they are treated and they won't go back to prison. I was a board member of this program in Bethel for many years. I helped create the court and the board supervised it to make sure it was working and doing what it was designed to do. It's not a traditional court in the sense that all it does is dispense punishment, but it has the aim of making these criminals successful when they come out and get back to society.

The goal is to fix lives. The Department of Corrections is destroying lives. It is called the Department of Corrections, but it should be called the Department of Punishment. There is a revolving door syndrome and so many Alaska Natives go to prison, get released, and go back in. Our jails are full of Alaska Natives. And most of the reason these Natives are filling the prisons has its origin in alcohol or drugs.

I was invited to speak to inmates in the jail in Bethel. To me it was more than just collecting signatures, but making war on alcohol in another way. I have also spoken to young people in schools about the ills of alcohol. I have done it in Akiak, Bethel, Tuluksak, and Kaltag. I talk to children about the issues of wellness and sobriety. I even did that on the Iditarod Trail in a village. I was trying to connect the signatures with the talk and connect it to the Iditarod. The kids were kindergarten through twelfth grades. I've done it in the Anchorage schools, too. It is the same message of wellness to all of them and how that relates to sobriety.

My thinking has not changed and if I were invited back to speak to inmates in jails and prisons I know what I would say. I would go, "Hey, all of you good prisoners in here, I would like to thank you for inviting me to speak to you today. What I have been doing with my Iditarod Trail Sled Dog Races is to bring attention to sobriety and there is a great and good reason why I have done this. I have lost six brothers to accidental deaths because they used alcohol and I know many of you are right here in this jail because of alcohol. If you were not using it you wouldn't be there because 95 percent of you have committed crimes while being drunk.

"Whatever your crime is, domestic violence, rape, I am pretty sure alcohol played a part in it. I am here to speak to you to say that we need to make changes in our lives, the lives of Alaska Natives, and you are the Alaska Natives. Our prisons in Alaska are full of Natives and that is you. That is you right here. What I would like to do is put the Department of Corrections out of business. They're in business to make money off of you and jobs are created and taxes are paid on account of you. The construction companies are building jails and they make good money out of those projects. The Department of Corrections has highly paid people here to watch over you, to feed you, to supply electricity, to clean the place. You guys are expensive and you are part of the economic development of the communities around you outside the walls. You guys are creating jobs for other people while you are miserable in here. You guys are just doing your time and getting worse as criminals while you are in the custody of the Department of Corrections.

"So my goal is for you to start thinking about what you can do to overcome that. I want you to overcome being in jail and being in the system. The Department of Corrections would love for you to come back to prison and would love to have you come back consistently so it can be paid to take care of you. But I'm here to tell you let's put the Department of Corrections out of business. I think you can help do it if you follow my advice and stay alcohol free and substance abuse free. When you get out of here, go out there and make something out of your life and learn from the mistakes that put you in here. That is the goal.

"You know we have been experiencing a lot of death in our villages, in our communities, and you know about that. People are committing suicide and you guys were committing crimes while using alcohol. We need to make changes. Our people have never been like that and they were never put in jails at such a rate as we have today. I am just trying to make little recommendations to help you. I am a prime example. I am an Alaska Native who has made a change in his life. I had problems with alcohol. You need to take advantage of your time while you are incarcerated. Get into an educational program. Do some research about what you can do with your life when you get out of here. Get your GED, if you have not gotten your high school diploma. You want to better yourself. Don't let your life waste away in here. Do something with your time while you are in prison.

"Try to get involved in improving your education. Get involved in some program or opportunity. If you can, try to get to a halfway house and get yourself back into the mainstream educational system. Or train to earn money and become independent. When you get out make plans to take care of yourself and be part of society. Give back to society that you are going into instead of creating more problems and employing the people who work for the Department of Corrections."

And that's generally the message that I give to the inmates.

I tell those inmates right away that I lost six brothers to alcohol. I think some of them do not believe me and think I am telling a lie. But the majority of them know what my story is, I think. They've heard about it.

The questions come after I stop speaking. They're always asking how I quit. How did I give up drinking? I tell them that I stopped drinking cold turkey. I decided to avoid drinking and I changed my friends to stay away from the friends that were using. I had a whole bunch of them. I changed friends to nondrinking friends. I also urge them to get more into spiritual activity, to get involved with a church. And I tell them to take up constructive activities like hunting and fishing. I emphasize to them that they have to keep busy when they get out of prison. They ask about me and they ask for recommendations: "How can I put my life back together?" They worry about the people they hurt in the village and they don't know how to reconcile their situation. They want to know how to make amends when they go back home.

It is different when I speak to the kids. They are younger and I am trying to head them off before they make poor decisions and get into trouble for the first time. I tell them a lot about the story of my life. I explain that I grew up in a small village and we grew up with sled dogs. I make sure they know I have run the Iditarod. I talk about how my family has always had dogs and how having sled dogs teaches responsibility. I tell them I tried to be a good student and listened to my parents and how especially my father was a big influence. I let them know they can make choices about what they do as they grow up.

I don't sugarcoat things, though. I tell them I understand that everyone growing up has different challenges. We have fear. We have issues of guilt. Sometimes we don't feel good about who we are. I also tell them stories my grandmother told me about living in the mountains in the old days and traveling from camp to camp to survive off the land. I think kids are really interested in those stories about their heritage.

And I admit that every village has its problems and young people have to be strong and stay away from making mistakes. They will see problems in their communities with drinking and with the use of drugs, and also cigarettes and tobacco. They need to do something else besides getting involved with these substances that can harm their health and mess up their lives. You will be offered these things, I tell them, but you need to refrain. When you are offered alcohol or drugs, you can say no. It takes courage to say no to the offers you will receive. But it is your choice whether or not to take these things and the right choice is to say no. It is your choice. It is your mind. It is your body. You have the right to say no. When little kids are involved I try to get the point across in ten or fifteen minutes and not ramble too much.

Something that helps me get the kids' attention when I visit a school is that I generally bring a lead dog from an Iditarod team with me. They are very interested in that dog and they pay attention to the story when I bring an animal with me. I speak to kids of all ages, but I try to keep them within age groups so I can speak to them appropriately. Sometimes it's just an entire school assembly, but I think it is better to visit them in their classrooms. It feels right to have a smaller group and kids of the same age together.

When I talk to older kids I go into more detail about the dangers and the consequences of abusing alcohol and drugs and I am firmer in my instructions to stay away. They are at a riskier age and they probably have been offered the chance to drink alcohol by that time in their life. I tell them to resist peer pressure. A lot of these kids have begun to slip into a depression because of what they see around them. We did some surveys in the schools on the issue of suicide and about eighty percent of the kids were sad or depressed and have thought about hurting themselves. The results were scary.

There are a lot of issues that are affecting Alaska Natives and some of them are universal and affect Native tribes in the Lower 48. I have been to conferences in a lot of places. I have been to events in Washington, D.C. quite often. I attended a conference in Tulsa, Oklahoma. I was at a conference in Reno, Nevada. I am on the Akiak Native Community Council. I am authorized to speak on the tribe's behalf. They give me permission to speak and present resolutions on Akiak's behalf about health care, education and justice issues, about climate change, natural resources, development, and the environment. I was the chairman of the Alaska Inter-Tribal Council for eight years between the mid-1980s and the mid-1990s. I am vice president for the National Congress of American Indians, which is based out of Washington, D.C. I have served with the International Indian Treaty Council. I have served for years.

I believe I have met President Obama three times. Each year in either November or December he meets with tribal leaders from throughout the country. Each of 565 is invited from Alaska and the Lower 48. The session is called the Tribal Nations Conference. This is backed by the White House, not the Bureau of Indian Affairs. There are 229 federally recognized tribes in Alaska. When he was in office, an executive order was issued by President Clinton that recognizes the ability of tribes to consult directly with the federal government.

President Obama said the purpose of our annual meeting is to strengthen the tribal nations—and we have to be strengthened. They tell you this is to give proper government status to the tribes equal to the federal government. When we sit down and meet we are sitting on a government-to-government basis. That's why all of the tribes are invited. The Akiak Native Community sent me as a delegate to represent Akiak. The president issued a statement saying he wanted to continue to meet with the representatives of tribal governments and that he wanted to meet face to face. They could not fit all of the tribal representatives into a meeting room at the White House so we have met at the Department of the Interior. Each time I was able to shake President Obama's hand. No other presidents have done that for us. This is the first president that has committed himself to meet with the tribal nation delegations.

Each time President Obama made a speech and after the speeches were done we have had the opportunity to spend time with the secretary of the interior, the secretary of energy, and other high-level cabinet members. We get to sit down and make our concerns known to the top secretaries in the government. David Hayes of the Interior said he would commit himself to respecting tribal sovereignty.

The president made the commitment to meet with tribal leaders during his campaign. He said if he was elected he would have meetings between the White House and the nation's tribal leadership. He kept his word. He's been doing it each year since he was elected to office.

It is valuable for us to meet with the high-level cabinet members to make our feelings and concerns known about the issues that affect us the most. There are plenty of ongoing issues in the Indian communities from health care to police protection, economic development, and more. We have been afforded the chance to bring grievances to government authorities. They say they will work to resolve issues with each tribe. We hope it turns out to be true.

CHAPTER 19

As people living in Alaska we are on the front lines of climate change. We see it happening all around us. The winters are not as severe as they were and winter comes later than it used to.

Now I am a member of the First Stewards Board, which is made up of members from Alaska, Natives from Hawaii, members from the Northwest United States near Seattle, a board member from the Great Lakes—I think from Wisconsin—a member from Arizona from a Southwest tribe, and a board member from the East Coast. The organization is pretty new. We had our first meeting in 2013 and it was formed to meet and discuss climate change that we are all experiencing.

We feel like we represent the first stewards of the lands of Alaska, North America, and the US Pacific islands with expertise and backgrounds in the lands and waters of the continent. Our ways of life are being impacted by climate change and we want to discuss it and have a say in policies the federal government passes.

Tribal governments agreed to form the First Stewards Board and I was one of the people involved in the start-up. Our chairman, Micah McCarty, is from the state of Washington. We began with a symposium and we heard witnesses talk about their experience in seeing climate change.

I became concerned about climate change when I first heard about villages that might have to relocate because of coastal changes. Newtok is in Western Alaska and some people have said those people are the first "refugees" in the United States because of climate change. I think Newtok is moving fifteen miles inland. The Yup'ik village of about 350 people is located below sea level and because climate change is causing permafrost to melt, the village could end up under water. The same is true of Kivalina and Shishmaref.

Anywhere the ice is melting in the Arctic where people live is causing the sea level to rise and the permafrost is going away because of global warming. A lot of Alaska villages are being slammed. Alaska is on the front line of global warming and Native villages seem to be impacted the most right now. Scientists have said that emissions from industry in places like the East Coast and the Midwest are getting into the air and drifting to the Arctic and melting the ice in the Arctic, as well as bringing all of those wonderful ingredients. What we are seeing in the Arctic Ocean is the disappearance of the permanent ice pack. That's why there is a threat to the future of polar bears. I think we are also seeing the effects on walrus and maybe on migratory birds. They depend on the ice. People are seeing more polar bears inland.

Of course it is very expensive to move whole towns. Some people say it will cost $200 million to $400 million and nobody wants to pay for it. It costs a lot of money to move a town with its infrastructure. This is a major policy issue: Who is going to pay? I attend the National Congress of American Indians meetings and events twice a year and that is an issue that is discussed. We have invited congressional delegations and we have tried to work with the National Oceanic and Atmospheric Administration and the US Corps of Engineers. I have given talks on climate change, too. I spoke in Washington, D.C.

There are so many issues that affect Alaska Natives. In 2013, Senator Mark Begich introduced into Congress the Alaska Safe Families and Villages Act to provide tribes the authority to enforce several state laws that revolve around criminal justice. I have concerns about where the state of Alaska stands on tribal issues, especially when it comes to areas of jurisdiction. I want there to be ways we can help protect our women and children in our villages. My worry was that the bill had no teeth because they removed the provision that let communities prosecute criminals. The problem is that the state will never allow the tribes to have full jurisdiction. They will never agree to that. So it's kind of watered down. It does some stuff, but in the end it's weak legislation. Senator Begich compromised too much with the state.

Congress passed the Violence Against Women Act and that recognized Indian country. It provides full faith and credit to the tribes. It gives tribes the right to adjudicate those offenses. President Obama signed that legislation in 2013. It will help strengthen tribes by giving them the ability to handle criminals in the communities whether the offenders are Natives or non-Natives. But there is only one Indian tribe in Alaska—in Metlakatla. The other 228 Alaska tribes are not covered. The rest of the tribes do not have Indian country.

This issue has been a big problem. It has been prevalent in the villages and it has exploded in Anchorage. Women are raped. They are victims of domestic violence. I believe that the underlying aspect of all of this violence against women is alcohol. That is why there is a need for the tribal governments to be given the authority. The other tribes in Alaska are part of Native Corporations and are under state law. The Native Corporations are under the jurisdiction of the state. Some villages barely have any police presence at all. State troopers are spread all over and they have huge areas they have to cover. They're too busy to take care of a lot of these crimes right away.

The Indian tribes around the country, plus Metlakatla, have the power, but the other Alaska tribes have no power and the state is doing nothing to help. The state of Alaska is not doing its job. The Alaska Safe Families and Villages Act could have removed the prohibition against the Alaska tribes to enforce the Violence Against Women Act the same way, but it did not.

This is the resolution I wanted: "Whereas all tribal sovereign nations on earth respect and hold sacred our women, our Native women, we retain our inherent right to regulate domestic relations for our women, children and families; and whereas Alaska is the home of 229 federally recognized tribes and there are over 200 rural Native villages in which federally recognized Indian tribes operate and only 78 of those are served by local trained state law enforcement;

"Whereas Alaska Native women suffer the highest rate of forcible sexual assault in the United States—an Alaska Native woman is sexually assaulted every eighteen hours, and according to the Alaska Native Tribal Health Consortium, one in two Alaska Native women experience physical or sexual violence in their lifetimes; and whereas geographical remoteness, extreme weather, and the lack of transportation infrastructure present challenges in responding to crime in Alaska Native villages and providing access to state judicial systems in a timely manner; and whereas Alaska Native women in urban areas are also threatened by physical and sexual violence; and whereas the state of Alaska continues to withdraw law enforcement resources from rural Alaska and Native women are increasingly at risk; and whereas federally recognized Indian tribes that operate within Alaska Native villages must be able to carry out local culturally relevant solutions to effectively address the lack of law enforcement in villages and the lack of access to swift state court proceedings; and whereas the National Congress of American Indians urged Congress to include protection to Alaska victims of sexual assault, domestic violence, dating violence and stalking in any final bill reauthorizing the Violence Against Women Act;

"Whereas the final version of the reauthorization of the Violence Against Women Act of 2013 contained 'a special rule for the state of Alaska' in which thereby applied sections of the Violence Against Women Act only to the Metlakatla Indian community and the Metlakatla Island Reserve; and whereas the National Congress of American Indians applauds the historic victories obtained for some tribes in the Violence Against Women Act of 2013, but also recognizing that the safety of Alaska Native women is still at risk; and whereas the Alaska Safe Families and Villages Act has been introduced in the 111th and 112th Congress by Senator Mark Begich.

"Now therefore be it resolved that the National Congress of American Indians supports the development of legislation that will 1) restore

Alaska Native village lands as Indian country with Alaska tribal governments having the same authority to address the needs of their people as the tribes of the Lower 48 and 2) at a minimum restore the authority of Alaska tribes to address domestic violence, dating violence and sexual assault within Native village lands as well as related problems with alcohol and drug abuse and 3) provide separate funding to Alaska tribal governments for necessary law enforcement in rural villages; and be it further resolved that the National Congress of American Indians supports the Alaska Safe Families and Villages Act and supports further amendment to expand the pilot project of Violence Against Women Act of 2013 to include all tribes in Alaska; be it finally resolved that this resolution shall be the policy of the National Congress of American Indians until it is withdrawn or modified by subsequent resolution."

That was approved at the National Congress of American Indians meeting in Reno, Nevada, in June of 2013.

If Congress was to pass that resolution into law we would need to start building jails in the villages. About eight years ago we filed a lawsuit to address the lack of law enforcement in the villages seeking equal protection. It won in the lower courts, but lost big-time in the Alaska Supreme Court. The court ruled that the Alaska Native villages are protected by the village public safety officers. We were asking to have a trained police force in every community instead of half-trained, lack-of-trained village officers. They cannot carry weapons. They have different uniforms. We were asking for certified police officers in each community. The lawsuit said that the state had the obligation to provide police protection just as it had the obligation to provide educational services. The villages are not afforded enough village police officers anyway. The state says it is because of budgetary constraints. We asked for two trained police officers per community. That would be a useful step. The state complained that it didn't have the $80 million it would have cost.

There is not even a village safety officer in every village, but I don't want a second-class police officer who is not certified. I would like to see police officers who go through training and have the authority to do investigations. They would carry weapons and they would have the ability to put people in jail. Right now with the village safety officers we live in the Old West. There is lawlessness. The village officer is just a helper for the state troopers. They cannot perform arrests. They can hold suspects until a state trooper arrives in the village.

The way it is now in 2014 is really a total lack of protection. It is the Wild, Wild West and criminals know they are going to get away with it, domestic violence and sexual assault. Some go to jail, but the problem is rampant and a lot of the guilty parties are running loose. It seems as if it pretty much takes murder or violent rape to get the state troopers to fly in. If there is a murder, they will show up. For domestic violence or sexual assault, maybe they will show up. That's my complaint. That's my concern. I hated like heck for Senator Mark Begich to introduce legislation that was supposed to catch us up with the Violence Against Women Act, but then have less for Alaska tribes in order to appease the state.

Former Governor Sean Parnell says the state of Alaska does not recognize the existence of tribes, the power of tribes. The governor has sole jurisdiction. No Alaska Natives were involved in the framing of the state constitution. The state of Alaska has not been living up to its responsibility. That has been my complaint about the state.

In Akiak we know there are some individuals who are committing a lot of crimes and children and women are hurt by these folks. We, as tribal governments, are sitting here wondering what to do. Sometimes we know someone has committed a rape. We try to work with the state troopers, but we're frustrated. We're sitting here without any authority given to us by Congress and the state of Alaska and our hands are tied. We are trying to exercise our sovereignty to defend our women and children. We are trying to work within our system, but the state troopers and the state courts do not support what we are doing.

Congress cannot believe it has dealt with us fairly because there is no Indian country for us. We don't qualify for money. I think if more people around the United States understood our situation they would be very angry. I have been outraged and when I am outraged I make statements. I'm a troublemaker. We need to educate other people about what goes on. The state of Alaska objects to a lot of the stuff involving tribal governments. The state does not want to give up any of its authority. When Tony Knowles was governor of Alaska we negotiated with the governor's office for a year and he issued an executive order saying that tribes do exist in Alaska. It's a statement. But it's not in the statutes. It's not law that he said it, so people can ignore his statement. It was a first step. But we have not been able to get other governors to do the same or more.

We're suffering in Alaska in the villages. The rest of Alaska, Fairbanks and Anchorage, should be indignant. But the majority of the legislature will never do anything to help the tribes. Republicans are in control and they would never be outraged. The average person should be outraged and that's what we need to work on, to tell our story over and over and over again. We are saying that these women and children have to be protected.

The tribes have fiduciary responsibilities and moral obligations to women and children. I think we are pursuing the right thing to do. A lot of the government policies are killing us. I think at the root a lot of these government folks are self-serving.

CHAPTER 20

Those major congressional acts that Senator Ted Stevens spear-headed were more valuable for the state of Alaska and for oil com-panies than they were for Alaska Natives. The Alaska Native Claims Settlement Act was geared to fail. It was set up to fail. Of course leaders of the corporations think that it was successful.

Alaska Natives have lost their lands. Younger generations have no standing. A lot of problems of rural Alaska stem from these situations. There are so many problems and I want to help with all of them so I serve on many boards. I was on the board of directors of the National Tribal Environmental Council, the Native American Rights Fund. I was on the State Board of Education. I was on the Governor's Advisory Board on Alcohol and Substance Abuse under Governor Wally Hickel. I was chair-man of the Yukon Kuskokwim Health Corporation Hospital Board. I'm also serving on the Rural Community Action program out of Anchorage. I'm currently serving on the Kuskokwim Management Working Group for management of Kuskokwim River fish. And I'm on the Akiak Native Community Tribal Council.

My son Mike says of me, "His phone rings a lot." I would say that is true. Plus, I am on e-mail and there are text messages. There is always a problem to work on. I worked to set up a suicide prevention conference in Anchorage in 2013. The Alaska Tribal Leaders Summit adopted a motto of "Securing Our Future for Our Children" and that is because so many young people are at risk. They are at risk because of alcohol and drugs, but that has also led to a more serious problem of suicides in the villages. There is no future if young people take their own lives.

The theme was supposed to be "addressing" the issue of suicide, but I like the word "arresting" because it means stopping suicides. Part of it was talking about what tribes can do to assist their young men and women live fuller, more hopeful lives. Since 1971, those born after December 18, 1971, have no rights to ownership of ancestral lands and are excluded from receiving shares of the corporation. It was their inheritance. The tribes need to address the challenge of healthy living for our children and grandchildren. It is an ongoing struggle to deal with non-functioning culture, dysfunctional families, parents in need of healing who lack parenting skills, exposure to substance abuse and violence, poverty, neglect in the home, lack of economic opportunity for the foreseeable future, boredom—nothing to do—hopelessness, powerlessness, fear, shame, guilt, neglect from the tribal government, and little pride. And people wonder why there are problems with suicides among young people in the villages.

The proportion of suicide for young people in the villages is way higher than it is throughout the rest of the United States and maybe the world. We are trying to figure out why. They were born without hunting and fishing rights. They were stripped of them. They have nothing left. There is hopelessness. They don't see a good future. Then they are surrounded by domestic violence, sexual assault, and the lack of enforcement against these predators. There is also a lack of adequate housing. Many people in villages are still living in Third World conditions in a state of dependency. The state of Alaska is wonderful in providing food stamps and programs like that to create dependency. Some people don't have to work. They can just get public assistance and live off of that and every month go to the store instead of feeding their families through subsistence hunting and fishing.

The top three causes of deaths in Alaska villages are cancer, accidental deaths, and suicide. Along the Kuskokwim River it is drownings, and a very high percentage of deaths involved drowning cases where alcohol was involved. In suicide cases, it's mostly the younger people and the Elders are burying the young. If I could speak directly to all of Alaska's Native young people, this is what I would say: "We have problems in our communities. We have to come to grips with it. We have to talk about it and see what we can do to avoid this killing machine. Policies from Washington, D.C., and the state of Alaska are geared to destroy all of us. Now that you are eating other foods diabetes is hitting our people big-time. You have to be careful what you eat. You're eating all of this junk stuff."

I would say, "You come from ancestors that did not have this problem. Their lives were whole and they did not kill themselves. They did not commit domestic violence. Those people who were born before you are living healthy lives and they're living long lives."

Young people have experienced rapid change. They have all of these wonderful computer games and they spend all of their time on them and are not getting out. They are basically not doing anything else. They are not hunting or fishing. They are not active. They are staying in the house and eating all of this sugar, chips, and drinking pop. We have to get back our identity and our language. It can be worked on. We also need to work on restoring our land to its rightful owners, so it will be secure forever. It is a message to the young people. Now the healthy older folks are burying the young folks and it should be the other way around.

I know it is difficult to make these types of arguments resonate in the heads of sixteen-year-olds who like to eat the junk food and play the games. But they have to listen, or else they're dead. It has to resonate. We have compiled a book of information about how Alaskan kids can succeed and every kid who is sad or suicidal should read it. We can't fix everything all at once, but we can try to address all of the problems.

Kids do have short attention spans and it is hard to get a message across that will help them tonight, this weekend, to change their thinking. We have to change policies or otherwise there is no hope for these kids. If they have a sense of hope they won't be depressed. Things are not well, but we need to have community leaders give a positive message to the kids. The leaders have to take stands. They can't lie down in the face of these problems. Tribal leaders need to stand up and say, "We're not going to take it anymore."

Our kids are killing themselves and we need to convince them that they are special and unique. For years they have been told by government policies that their way of life is no good. We need to change to a better society. We cannot be somebody else. We cannot be a white guy. We have to be who we are. We have lost so much. I have to believe that most kids that are going to kill themselves are sending signals. We need to identify those and go in and get them into a structured environment. I've done that many times—to intervene. As a counselor I have been doing that for many years. We need to put them in an environment to watch them 24/7 and make sure they are safe right now. That's the easy part, to prevent them from shooting themselves or hanging themselves right now. Then we talk to them. We need to convince each of them that he is a special person, that he can get an education, and that things will get better. The pride of identity is a big part of it.

We have gotten better over the last few years at seeing warning signs and intervening right away. In Akiak, we conducted a healing circle where we talked about the issue of the community in a closed setting where the word would not get out. We do not talk about what was discussed outside of the room. We deal with the issues in the hearing circle. What you say in the hearing circle stays in there and it is not to be shared anywhere else. It is a safe, trusting environment where you can let things out. It is part of the healing process. Now we have a hearing circle once a week for two hours.

Last night when we met there we talked about two boys. We talked about protection of them. You need to keep talking. The underlying causes, that's the difficult part. But we can try to fix the symptoms right now. In these meetings we are trying to flush out the concerns and the worries. We have both Elders and youths in there. A suicide is a community disaster. It takes a long time to heal and I don't think it ever heals. I compare it to losing my six brothers to alcohol. It is still in my mind. Even though something happened ten years ago or thirty years ago it is still not fixed. Losing my brothers was a disaster. I'm still working on it. I do some positive work, but it is still a wound that is open.

It is not very different from a Hurricane Sandy disaster or a Katrina disaster. How can you heal from a disaster in a short time? I'm not going into this with my eyes closed.

Climate change is now coming to Akiak in a way that is tangible. We are seeing a lot of erosion on the Kuskokwim River. The old village of Akiak is in the middle of the river right now. One summer we had to move the grave site. The cemetery was moved inland. This has been going on for thirty years, gradually. I know when we bury our dead the permafrost is getting thinner. It seems like it is receding every year. We might be another of those villages like Newtok, Kivalina, and Shishmaref that could see the banks of the river wash away and force us to move.

When we moved the graves a lot of people got sick from the human remains for some reason. It's just hard dealing with bones and carefully moving them and seeing skulls. That was the hardest job our young men did. But we moved the remains to a new burial site.

As a subsistence fisherman and someone who is catching fish for the kids, I am out on the river all of the time. It used to be that we had to set fish traps under the ice earlier. The timing of our ability to get lush fish was changing and we missed out until later. The ice was thinner longer and the river was open longer, even to Thanksgiving. Some years we were able to boat on the river up until Thanksgiving. That got my attention. I started looking into it and reading reports from international meetings. Everybody was giving out reports about the impact of global warming on the Pacific Ocean, Alaska, the Bering Sea, and the Gulf of Alaska. People were seeing more frequent storms and the ice up north was receding.

It became clear that some Alaska villages were in jeopardy just like the polar bear and the walrus. We were vulnerable communities and we had to notify the world. I began to get more interested and it seems likely that climate change will eventually affect 180 villages in Alaska. That's how many communities seem at risk of being under water in fifty years. Akiak is one of them. The emissions are all spewing out of cars and going up into the air and then the stuff comes down. We're feeling it and the indigenous people are getting the effects of greenhouse gas emissions in many places.

Winter is coming later and it is affecting our lives through our subsistence activities. Going back to the 1960s things were normal. After the 1970s things seemed to change rapidly. I began listening to the Elders talk about the weather. They talked about the weather every single day and they predicted the weather. We joke about how the weather service is always wrong. The Elders make fun of them. They say, "Gee whiz, I wonder why those weather folks are never fired for being incompetent."

For generations the Elders talked about the weather, made observations, predicted salmon runs, read the winds. When they saw a wind pattern change they wondered if there were going to be good runs of salmon in the winter. I think climate change has a psychological effect on our people, too. People in Akiak are experiencing anxiety because of the erosion affecting their homes. I have seen the loss of sixty feet of embankment in one year. Sixty feet of land went into the water.

In 2007, I testified in Congress before the Select Committee on Energy Independence and Global Warming. The topic was "Energy and Global Warming Solutions for Vulnerable Communities." We have those vulnerable communities in Alaska, for sure.

At the time I was vice chairman of the Akiak Native Community, vice chairman of the Alaska Inter-Tribal Council, and vice president of the National Congress of American Indians, and a board member of the National Tribal Environmental Council. This was part of my testimony: "Global warming is undermining the social identity and cultural survival of Alaska Natives and American Indians. As we watch our ice melt, our forests burn, our villages sink, our sea level rise, our temperatures increase, our oceans acidify, and our animals become diseased and dislocated, we recognize that our health and traditional ways of life are at risk. Our Elders, in particular, are deeply concerned about what they are witnessing. In Alaska, unpredictable weather and ice conditions make travel and time-honored subsistence practices hazardous, endangering our lives.

"Lakes are drying, new insects are appearing, permafrost is melting, berries are disappearing, storms are fiercer, animal populations are changing, our fish are rotting on drying racks, and polar bears are drowning."

I believe that Alaskans can be part of the solutions—and American Indians, as well—with economic opportunities in a low-carbon future, especially with respect to renewable energy. In Alaska we are installing wind power in very remote communities, such as Tooksok Bay, St. Paul Island, and Kotzebue. Port Graham village is assessing construction of a biomass facility using forestry waste. Wind power has also been installed on the Rosebud Sioux Indian Reservation. To achieve Indian country's and Alaska's renewable energy potential, we need investment capital, infrastructure, and technical capability. It always comes down to money.

A few years ago I made a speech about climate change at a National Congress of American Indians convention. I was convinced this was a new threat to us. I thought the evidence was real and that this change might be the greatest challenge facing humanity today. Climate change is destabilizing plant and animal habitats and disrupting relationships within them. Some species are shifting northward and upward in elevation. Invasive species are coming in their place. Local landscapes are changing, soils are drying, lake and river levels are declining. Native foods and fisheries are declining. Tribal access to traditional foods and medicines is becoming limited as a result of reservation boundaries. That is why I say that tribal people are impacted by climate change more severely than other peoples.

We tribal leaders, our Elders, our people, our youth, must rise to the challenge. Because of our traditional knowledge, our intimate understanding of our lands, our respect and love for Mother Earth, we can take on a leadership role in the world's efforts to address this monumental crisis. Peoples from all over the world are asking for our help. We have unique knowledge to help them and to help ourselves. Through our practices and knowledge we have survived and thrived for thousands of years. These practices are nature-based, time-tested, and climate resilient. We are the first "natural resources managers." If we choose, we can share this message with the world, which is now clamoring to hear it and understand it. So after five hundred years of bad treatment of our peoples and practices, many in this world are realizing just how important our knowledge is.

When presidential candidates were talking about cutting the

amount of carbon emissions, a presenter at a National Congress of American Indians convention said that "climate change and activities have the potential to create more revenue for tribes than gaming does now." There are many existing federal programs that can provide funding for certain things that will help with global warming. We are on the verge of a Green Revolution. Tribal traditional knowledge can be preserved and carried on to the next generations.

I attended a climate meeting in Anchorage and there were stories from Hawaii and Guam about rising water levels. These things are happening to indigenous nations around the world. There are bigger storms wiping out cities and towns. The rising water is affecting villages. There were those terrible tornadoes in Oklahoma. The lawmakers are asked to fund relief in New York and New Jersey because of Sandy and in Oklahoma and they don't want to do it. Some of them are the same lawmakers who say global warming isn't happening.

Someone might ask why I am interested in climate change because I already have enough to do, serve on enough boards, and take on so many issues. But to me they are all intertwined relating to the condition of the people. The climate change is part of the conditions they live with, the anxiety, and the changes in subsistence habits. They are facing anxiety that they might lose their homes or community infrastructure. When those folks in Shishmaref move it will affect their hunting and fishing patterns. That all has an adverse effect on the mind. It is all stress.

It is natural to wonder what will happen. That is the unknown. And because it is so expensive to relocate a village the state and federal governments don't want to pay for it. But the people will have to move sometime or else they will be under water.

To me all of the problems are connected in terms of survival. All of these issues concern rapid change. For thousands of years our people were complete and survived on their own. Now all of these rapid changes are intertwined, from the migration of animals changing, to fishing patterns, to weather. These things have an effect socially and psychologically for people.

Climate change is an extra concern. We already had so many other problems. Who needed that, too? But we cannot escape that. It is part of the change we are experiencing up north. We have to deal with more than one problem at a time. If climate change was going to make a big impact on a big city right away Congress would probably jump in and mitigate it, come up with some kind of adaptation plan quickly and fund it. Not in the North in our villages. Congress poured billions of dollars into New Orleans to try to prevent flooding. They poured billions of dollars into California to rebuild from wild fires and mud slides. But in our communities there is no money, nothing, zero.

CHAPTER 21

To me, the fact that Alaska Native tribes do not have Indian country is a huge thing. If Alaska villages were considered to be Indian country I think it would protect our lands in perpetuity. The Native corporations are for-profit and of course the Venetie case that was decided by the US Supreme Court ruled that the corporation lands are not Indian country.

That was one of the biggest government losses we ever had. When the Alaska Native Claims Settlement Act passed, the secretary of the interior quit taking land into trust in Alaska. What that means is that Alaska tribes are denied protection of our lands. The only community that has lands in trust is Metlakatla. That is the only place in Alaska that chose not to go along with the Alaska Native Claims Settlement Act. They didn't agree with it and they said no as a tribe. They chose to continue to put their lands in trust with the secretary of the interior of the federal government. They were the only ones.

Some people thought they were crazy at the time going so much against the grain. But in Metlakatla they foresaw the long-term effect to know that hunting and fishing rights were extinguished and understood how it affected kids born after December 18, 1971. I think Metlakatla was the smart one. Now their lands are in trust and they have Indian country. Whenever Congress passes legislation that discusses Indian country relevant to the Indian nations throughout the United States, Metlakatla is included. They receive the full benefits when laws like the Violence Against Women Act go through. They are eligible for funding.

It seems illogical that all of the Indian tribes in the United States except Natives in Alaska are considered Indian country. In my opinion it is against the constitution of the United States to exclude any of the tribal lands. Throughout the Lower 48 one of the most unusual byproducts of Indian country is that there is so much casino gambling. I suppose that if Alaska tribes had Indian country there would be casinos in Alaska. That would be up to the Indian Gaming Commission. There would not be 228 casinos, but every tribe would have the right to apply.

My thinking is that if you are sovereign the federal government has no business regulating the tribes and telling us what we can and cannot do. We would be able to provide all of the laws and deal with starting projects that could benefit our tribal citizens in each community. As far as casinos go, some tribes would want them and others would not. But it is a myth that just because a tribal nation has a casino that it is rich. That is just like because we have Alaska Native corporations in Alaska with billions of dollars, everybody in the tribe is rich. That is a myth, too. The money does not trickle down to everybody. Plus there are those 70,000 to 80,000 children who were deprived of benefits. The shareholders get dividends, but what can you do with $300 or $600 in a year to make a difference?

What the tribes can do—and we've seen that in the South 48—is that they can start businesses and they are not all casinos. The tribal governments are nonprofit organizations. They have tax status as Indian country. For many years tribes in the United States lived in poverty and many still are living in poverty. In Alaska many of our tribes barely exist and have no money.

Some tribes and Native corporations are starting to get into the tourism business. Where the land is managed by the village or a regional corporation they are trying that. We could do that in Akiak, I guess.

There is free money through tourism departments that might let us get started. People could visit and go out on the river and eat Native foods. We have talked about it. In Akiak we look at the opportunity for fishing. We could sell it as . . . Come to Akiak and fish in a wild river, the Kuskokwim. We would build a couple of cabins upriver for lodging and then go to tourism fairs with the slogan, "This is what you can do in Akiak." I think there is tourism starting in Southeast Alaska and up north the people do Eskimo dances for tourists and they're doing it in Barrow. There is limited tourism in Bethel. There are a lot of rich people who want to take what they consider to be exotic vacations and if they are treated well money does not seem to be an object.

It would help if the forty-four million acres of our lands that was transferred to the Native corporations could be transferred to tribal governments so we could practice our own jurisdiction. I would be happier if the lands became Indian country and the people were united for economic purposes. We need capital. In some endeavors you have to own the land to start a business.

If you are Indian country you could get the benefits of working with the Small Business Administration. There are opportunities to obtain capital through the Department of Commerce if you are Indian country. Right now we're a tribal government with no land. If we want to build houses we have to beg village corporations for land to build the houses on. The corporation shareholders own the land.

When it comes to tourism and bringing people to Akiak, I am definitely someone who knows what the travel challenges are. I fly a lot and do business in Washington, D.C., quite often. It takes me a day and a half to get there. I fly from Akiak to Bethel, then fly from Bethel to Anchorage, then from Anchorage to Seattle and from Seattle to Washington, D.C. The round-trip fare costs about $2,000.

I travel to wherever the tribal nations gather for conventions. I want to be there. There are workshops on the issues of alcohol, education, and other matters and the highest cabinet members are in attendance. You have the opportunity to meet with federal officials who have power to do things. I have also been to many Indian reservations in the South 48 to observe the quality of life. A lot of them have nothing, zero.

They were very poor. They had no economic development. A lot of them then started in with casinos and they had an income. Going back to them after they were recognized as Indian country it was like night and day. Many of them have improved the conditions in their homes. Some have started museums to help preserve the language and culture. There are still many needy tribes, though. Again, not every tribe has a casino and not every tribe is rich. A lot of them are still in poverty and in need of financial help to deal with issues. We see that in Alaska. Some people do believe that because of the Native corporations all Natives are rich. Not all Native corporations are equal and many village corporations are on the verge of going bankrupt. Being an Indian or an Alaska Native can be challenging in ways that white communities never experience.

One thing that has sustained me through difficult times is my religion. I am a Christian. I believe in God and I grew up going to church and going to Sunday school every Sunday. My great-grandfather was one of the first here to accept and adopt Christian religion after looking it over. The people ended up translating the Bible from Genesis to Revelations into Yup'ik. I have been involved with working with young people in the church and serving on our church council for as long as I remember.

At the Iditarod banquet in Anchorage before the start of the race each year I have been called upon to say a few words in prayer to the thousand or so people gathered there. I think I have done it three or four times. The Iditarod Trail Committee asked me. Joanne Potts in the Iditarod offices got in touch with me. She knew I wouldn't say no. I leave it up to God for me to decide. If he asks me, then I will do it.

I pray to God in English and Yup'ik for the safety of the mushers, to give them strength, to guard against serious accidents and for the mushers to be protected. I also pray for the villages to be safe and thank the Creator for allowing us to go through the land he created and for the wonderful opportunity he has given us to see his wonderful work. I pray for all of the mushers to make it to Nome safely and if they do not make it for them to be commended for what they tried to do. I am mainly thanking the Creator and praising him for allowing this to happen in Alaska and for providing us with the dogs we need to go along this trail.

Whether I am in church or somewhere else I always pray every day. I start the day with the Lord's Prayer, thanking him for the day he has given us. Then I ask God to give me the guidance to address the issues that affect my people and give me the strength to work on the problems and to run dogs and run the Iditarod. I ask God to allow me to accomplish those tasks. Although sometimes I have questions about faith, sure enough he makes things happen to fall into place.

My faith has been tested when all of those horrible things were happening to my brothers. I did blame God for a few years. I asked, "Why are you doing this to me?" And I blamed them. As my brothers passed away one after the other I asked, "Why are you allowing this to happen?" I asked God, "If you are God and if you love the people here, why are you allowing these bad things to happen in my life?" I questioned him, but I believe it was a mistake on my part to blame God for the bad things that happened in my life to my family.

I came around. I went, *Hey, wait a minute, Mike. God allows these things to happen, these bad things, and we are not immune to them. He allows these things to happen, but he will always care for us and in turn help us recover.* And he does. I did hit a low point in my faith. I think it was a very tough test for me. I should have read the Bible a couple of times from beginning to end. I thought of Job, the guy who had everything, but God allowed the bad guy to test him. He had family, riches, everything, but in the end he lost everything and his health was affected. Satan said, "I want you to curse God." He never did. He did not succumb to that test by the Devil. I kept thinking about that. He suffered, but he never lost his faith and he never succumbed to cursing God. I looked at that and felt I had made a mistake in blaming God for all of my wounds and for the condition of my family. Job did not succumb to cursing God and he was restored his riches and his family. He got everything back again and even more so.

That was the story that I looked at. I kept reading Job and that helped me as a person. I began blaming that guy, the Devil, who had been going around in our communities with the evil spirit that attacked us through the vehicle of alcohol and other things.

After that I think I emerged stronger. During that period when all of my brothers died because of alcohol-related accidents, what really saved me and kept me from going insane was the Bible, reading all of the stories right up to the end. I applauded the strength that God gave me through the history, the Old Testament and the New Testament. Looking at them, all of the stories, I see we as human beings will go through a lot and that we are not immune from persecution. We are not immune to bad things happening to us.

When the Elders looked at the Bible and read the Ten Commandments, they said that they had also been taught the same rules. Those were the rules of life in Yup'ik society even before contact. When they compared what they were taught and the Bible they realized they were similar. We were taught to integrate our ways of doing things with white civilization. I know that the Jewish people are still waiting for the Messiah, that he is still outstanding. But we believe that Jesus Christ is the Messiah and he died for our sins.

I believe I am here for a purpose, but I still remember what the Elders of the past who have gone away already have taught me and what my religion has taught me. Many Elders made time to counsel me and teach me. They had something to say, some concerns about the future, and I remember they told me I had to have strong faith. They emphasized that we have got to love everybody and no matter what the greatest thing I did was, it had to be done with love and concern. I also spent a lot of time with Bishop Jacob Nelson, who is in his late eighties now, and lives in Bethel. He is a longtime pastor who went village to village. Phillip Charley Sr. was another guy who came around. They talked to me about being strong for our people and strong for our ways of life. All of the spiritual leaders said we had to protect the land.

I try to pass all of these thoughts on to young people when I speak to them one-on-one and when I make speeches at schools and churches and in community meetings.

After the dark period of doubt for me I came out with my faith strengthened and the will to continue living and believing that in the end things are going to work out in God's favor. I really believe that even though we go through trials and tribulations and suffering. I look at the Israelites being captive in Egypt and then they were allowed to leave and go to the Promised Land. They went through a lot and it took forty years of wandering in the wilderness.

The way I am looking at it maybe the Alaska Natives are wandering in the wilderness now and that there is a land of milk and honey for us and we will get to the Promised Land. We're going to go through periods of division, and then periods of making false gods, a period of doubt and division and then faith will take over. There have been people in government that wanted to wipe us out, but God has protected us every step of the way. Look at what Moses was able to do. Against all odds, he succeeded. We are going to get to the Promised Land, too. Actually, we are in the Promised Land. We just don't own it.

CHAPTER 22

Akiak is a small community and that brings us all together. We have birthday parties for our young ones, two, three years old and the door is open to anyone in the village to come and eat. We have celebrations when youngsters catch their first fish or hunt their first migratory bird. We have festivals and everyone is welcome. It has been done forever that way. When special events occur everyone can come and celebrate together. We have community feasts and birthday feasts.

We had a birthday party for my four-year-old granddaughter. It was a smaller one, mostly family. We only had about fifty people stop in. Usually, it is a big feed and everybody comes. My mom did the same thing with me. Every birthday I looked forward to having everybody in the community come to our house and I was happy that we did that. You don't see that in big cities, but it does happen in Anchorage, at least for all family and friends to be invited.

When I was young, my grandmother Elizabeth Williams used to tell me stories all of the time. Some of them were the usual fairy tales like "Jack and the Beanstalk" in Yup'ik. But others were Native folk tales. There was one about a big-mouthed baby and that scared me a little bit.

We do not have paved roads in Akiak and most of the people who have vehicles rely on four-wheelers. Almost every household has a four-wheeler. The posted speed limit for the village is thirty miles per hour and that is fine for gravel roads. There may be children playing in the streets. Every household has a snowmachine for winter. It costs about $7 to buy a gallon of gas in Akiak. Yep, seven bucks. The cost of fuel oil is also about $7.

The first school we got when Molly Hootch was settled is now a storage building. We have a much newer school that is modern and cost $14 million. The money came from the state. We spent fifteen years advocating for the need for a new school. We lucked out. We have K through twelve all in one building. The water and sewer system was installed by the community.

Houses are built on pilings now because sooner or later the Kuskokwim River is going to flood. It does with some regularity in the spring. Once in while it is worse and the water moves inland a bit. For those whose geography is fuzzy, we are not close to the Arctic Circle and we have a lot of trees. In front of the school there is a greenhouse that is mostly made from aluminum and sealed tight against cold weather. Our airport is only a gravel strip and the planes are all two- or four-passenger prop planes.

The weather is not as harsh as some people think. Yes, it can be minus forty degrees, but it can warm up in January and rain instead of snow sometimes. In January, with the windchill, it can be minus 100 one day and 40 degrees above the next day.

Akiak has a small grocery store. When a visitor comes and asks if there is sticker shock because of the prices, I say, "You'll see for yourself." Here are some of the costs: $3.50 for a twenty-ounce soda. A fifteen-ounce jar of mayonnaise costs $6.35. A ten-ounce bag of Lay's potato chips cost $8.75. They have canned goods, not homegrown vegetables. My guess is that the prices are triple what they are in Anchorage because of transportation costs and Anchorage's costs are higher than almost anywhere else in the Lower 48.

One day there was a sign on the wall in the grocery store that said because of vandalism at the water plant there would be no fresh water for a day when repairs were made. That meant we could not flush our toilets or get water from the faucet. A few children broke into the water house, but they were caught. We definitely don't want to go back to packing water in buckets to each house.

The cost of human food in the grocery store is emblematic of the difference in cost in what it takes to be a musher in rural Alaska compared to living on the road system. We do make bulk orders from the chain warehouse stores in Anchorage for things. Wal-Mart has free shipping. We did make catalog orders, too. One thing that has changed and made our lives easier is the computer. We don't buy from catalogs the way we did. We do our ordering from Amazon. If we need something we Google it and go from there ordering anywhere in the world. My wife and I are sort of old school and we usually phone in orders, but Mike Jr., Shawna, and Sheila do that on the computer all of the time.

There may be quirks to daily life, but for me, it is still worth it to live in a small community in the Alaska Bush. The flip side is it is quiet. It is laid-back. We can go out fishing and hunting with our relatives, most of whom are right here. We have extended family here together. You can go out whenever you feel like going out. Out the back door the wilderness is maybe a hundred yards away. You're not fighting traffic. You know a lot of people—almost everybody in the community. This is all the other side of the high cost of living. These are the benefits.

We had a much simpler life when I was a boy. They had big candlelight services for Christmas in Bethel and my friend Willie and I would go with a couple of dog teams. That was a treat from mom and dad to let us go. We were between twelve and fifteen years old. I loved to go to the movies. They had movies at the community center that cost ten cents. There were a lot of Tarzan movies and John Wayne. Some of them were Charlie Chaplin comedies. Sometimes we just went to Akiachak to visit—it was only eleven miles away. We didn't have sports activities when we were young, not like they have today. Now we have basketball games, Native Youth Olympics events, dog races, community dinners, gatherings, and fiddle dances. It's not all doom and gloom.

Going back to my boyhood, dog mushing was always important. I helped take care of the dogs in the lot and I was able to drive teams between villages when I was a teenager. But when the racing started and I was working with Walter we had a lot of fun. One person who was a big influence on me was George Attla. George is the greatest sprint musher of all time. He won the Fur Rendezvous ten times. And he had to face adversity. He got tuberculosis and had a fused, stiff leg so he couldn't run. He did the first Iditarod, too, and finished fourth even though he was not a long-distance guy.

Walter and I first met George during the musher meetings for the Rendezvous. We would have the drawing and I went up and introduced myself. Walter bought some dogs from him so we could interbreed our dogs with his Indian dogs. The guy was the best in the world. We had dogs from Akiak that had tough feet and good fur. They could withstand anything in our area to do a job for my father, but I felt if we could connect with George's breed of dogs from Huslia and those villages we would probably see an improvement in their stamina and speed, especially their speed. So we figured why not go to the top? We were successful breeding his dogs to our dogs and that's how we got really started in mushing. Later, if I was in Fairbanks I would make sure to visit George in North Pole. We talked about breeding and feeding and training.

George gave me a lot of encouragement. It's a tough sport. It's a tough life, but the focus is always on the health of the dog, the conditioning, and the nutrition. He was one of the first ones that I tapped for recommendations and continuous information. I always wanted to hear how he came from the village and won and kept winning for a long period of time. George was willing to take his team to the Lower 48 and compete in Minnesota, Michigan, and those big races. I knew he was committed to being a champion and overcoming the adversity of his disability.

He bettered my breed and the first breeding with his dogs really helped and our kennel seemed to speed up. That breeding with George's hounds and our tough dogs was a very good combination. I also got to meet Gareth Wright, Roxy Wright, Charlie Champaine, and Doc Lombard, who was at the end of his career, while we were at the Rendezvous. I hung out with Charlie a lot. Our dogs were about the same speed then and afterwards I would watch him feed his dogs chicken and beef. He had a different style of feeding. He fed them store-bought, human-grade chicken and beef. I thought, *Gee whiz, I can't afford that.*

It was very expensive, but maybe he got some sponsors. We talked a lot about dogs. All of those guys seemed pretty happy that there was some village participation. They liked the idea someone was coming from Akiak to compete in the world championships. They were always interested in the kind of dogs we had and what we did. Their dogs were speedsters and after a while they said, "Oh, Mike those dogs seem to be built to run in the Iditarod." My first reaction was that I didn't think of them that way. The Iditarod seemed to be too much work, too far, and I didn't have that kind of time to train them and the kind of money I needed to enter.

Young people especially don't remember this, but before the Iditarod came along and during the early years of the Iditarod, the Rendezvous was *the* event. It was on the radio and it was televised and everybody in Alaska would be watching. There was also a lot of betting going on—not officially. The Rondy was the biggest thing happening in Alaska. I'm glad we were part of it then. My dad supported me and Walter. He would say, "Go and compete with those guys and see what you have. With experience you will learn to compete against the best in the world." We did that and would come back here and Walter would run the local races and he won all of the time.

I also got friendly with the Redingtons through the Fur Rendezvous. Joee would race, Raymie would race sometimes, and Timmy would race consistently. So I got to know them and Joe Redington Sr. would come around. Of course, Earl Norris was around. These guys had been around dogs for a long time and had good histories. After a while we also tapped into Gareth Wright's breeding with the Aurora huskies. Meeting Joe Redington was interesting. I made time to visit him in Knik. I called him up and told him how interested I was in the dogs he was racing. I visited with Joe and his wife, Vi, and picked his brains about what led him to start the Iditarod. He was always there and welcoming. At that time he had about three hundred dogs, which of course was a huge dog lot. But the interesting thing was once when I was at the house they also had about thirty cats. I think they were Vi's pets.

Part of it, I think, was that Joe had lots and lots of dog food and that attracted mice, so they let the cats take care of that problem. I became good friends with Raymie while visiting out there. Raymie was one of the people that urged me to do the Iditarod. That led to Walter trying the Iditarod in 1983. We finally broke down and said, "Why don't we try this?" Walter did it after we talked about it for ten years.

I learned more about dogs talking to Lester Erhart—there have always been members of the Erhart family doing the Rondy—and Carl Huntington was there. He wasn't as receptive to talking, but he is the only musher to win the Rendezvous and the Iditarod. Most mushers are very generous with information and they want to see younger people succeed. I think the information sharing has greatly improved the breed of dogs in the Iditarod.

I became friendly with Susan Butcher when she came to race in the Kusko 300 every year. She put in a good word for me with Lynden Air Cargo, which has helped me as a sponsor over the years. I ended up buying some of Susan's dogs to breed with mine. Walter and I became good friends with Rick Swenson, too, when he came to Bethel for the Kusko.

My Rendezvous experience, and the people we met, was huge preparation for doing the Iditarod. I wish there was more mingling now. I saw that in recent years a few mushers switched over and tried the Rendezvous, Jeff King, Lance Mackey, Libby Riddles, Jack Berry. A long time ago the goal was to do well in the Rendezvous and do well in the Iditarod. Now they are different specialties. Walter always wanted to win. He dreaded coming in second. He hated that. One time he finished second in a race in Kwethluk and he took the trophy and threw it in the trash can. Maggie and I picked it up. I lectured him about it. I told him he needed to be more respectful even if he wanted to win every race. "Doing second is not bad." He did that in public, too, and everybody was just shocked. They said, "What the heck is he doing?" He was a hard-core competitor and above all he wanted to win the Kusko, but he didn't. He came in third and fourth a bunch of times. It is still a goal in my family. We have come close a bunch of times. I think if my brothers were still alive and I didn't have the stress from their deaths that we would have achieved it by now.

They're all gone and I keep racing. No matter where I finish, I am happy with what I am doing. Mike Jr. has won races of fifty miles and he was second in the Kusko. Those are reasons to celebrate, to feel good. Those are accomplishments. He is much quieter than Walter. Walter would say, "I'll kick your ass when you come to town, George Attla." He told Myron Angstman, Susan Butcher, and Rick Swenson, "I'm gonna whoop your ass when you champions come around. I didn't train for nothing." He was blunt, a joker type guy, and sometimes I wished that he didn't run his mouth. But he was outspoken and didn't care who heard him. I tried to mellow him down, but it was a hard job. Mike Jr. is quiet and easygoing and you don't know what he is thinking most of the time. He is reserved and doesn't say much. Even I have to ask him to talk. But he's been winning, winning, winning these local races. He has been doing it consistently, quietly creeping up on the best mushers.

I have tried to be a good role model in Akiak with my mushing the Iditarod and carrying the sobriety signatures and the community has really supported me. When I talk to the kids they seem to appreciate the mushing. Now with Mike Jr. showing them what is possible he can help them feel good about who they are, too. It's a positive thing to have role models that are sober and strong and that advocate for good things to happen to the village.

All of the work and effort I have put into solving problems over the years, some people outside of Alaska and outside of the tribal world noticed. I have cooperated with people that wrote books because I thought it would be fresh ways to bring attention to the issues of concern. A woman named Jane Painter wrote a book called *Champions for Change: Athletes Making a World of Difference* and there was a chapter about me. She wrote about athletes who are trying to make a difference and change the world. I was speaking about climate change and I think that is why she picked me and how she found me.

I was part of another book, too, called *Asserting Native Resilience: Pacific Rim Indigenous Nations Face Climate Change*. It makes you hope that your message is getting out there. It was done by Zoltan Grossman of Evergreen College in the state of Washington. It is about the resilience of indigenous peoples. There is a chapter about me and a speech I made to a congressional committee on climate change. The topic was vulnerable communities because of climate change. I was surprised to get a call from people asking about my story.

These people are not really calling me because I am an Iditarod musher, but because I am involved in these issues, these problems, and trying to fix things. A lot of these other athletes are using their sport for a forum for change, too. Some are feeding the hungry. They all have causes they put time into, things they are advocating for. A lot of them are stretching their necks out for a cause like I have been doing. I still have my head. It hasn't rolled.

In fact, there is a Giraffe Award that is given out through an organization founded in 1984 by a woman who lived in New York. It is actually called The Giraffe Heroes Project and it focuses on support for people who stick their neck out and take risks for good causes. DeeDee Jonrowe nominated me for it. It is supposed to draw attention to people that are basically unknown who are trying to do important things with their time and energy. I guess I am a giraffe, but no, we don't have a giraffe mixing in with the dogs in the kennel.

Given what I do with all of the boards and councils I work with, a computer is a necessity. It has become an irreplaceable tool for me to communicate about climate change, the Violence Against Women Act, and other issues. I am living here in Akiak and the world is out there. It makes communication with any government agency in the state or in Washington, D.C., convenient. You're connected to the world here. I have communicated with Senator Begich's office and Senator Lisa Murkowski's office from my office here on my kitchen table.

It has been just over two years that we have had wireless. Growing up we didn't even have television for a long time. My dad finally got us a TV. For a while there was one TV in the village and everyone went and watched that. It was not so long ago that we had one telephone and it was in my office. Everybody lined up to make phone calls to wherever they had to and then people started getting phones and calling cards. Then cell phones came around. Now everybody has a cell phone here, even my grandkids. I can text them and tell them to come home. The technology is amazing. It has greatly improved in the last ten years. The Alaska Bush is connected.

Now I do all of my travel arrangements from here for hotels, car rentals, and planes. I have instant communications with the organizations I work with. If something goes wrong we report it to GCI and they fix it even if we are very remote. They are pretty efficient. Technology has shrunk the world for us. I think I have around two thousand friends on Facebook. Of course I can't really keep up with them all. I can communicate with my friends in Hawaii. I have friends in Chicago. I have friends on the East Coast. My children are more advanced than I am and my grandson Ray, who is thirteen, definitely has more technological skills than I do. He knows the computer inside-out. Ray will help me when I need it.

We had an emergency meeting in Akiak and we texted the information out to the community to tell residents when and where it was and what the agenda was. People showed up and they knew what we were going to talk about. The other day a lady at my office in Akiak wanted to get some information about a contact in Washington, D.C., and needed it fast. In the old days we would play tag with phone calls or snail mail and it would be shipped in a week and we would get the information in two weeks. Now we e-mail and by the end of the day she had it.

CHAPTER 23

Some of my favorite times outside of work have been going on hunting and fishing trips for food. Sometimes I went with friends and sometimes with family. But there are times when things happen in the outdoors that can be dangerous.

One time I almost drowned on the Kuskokwim River when I got thrown out of a boat while fishing with our nets. The boat was sliding sideways on the river and it came to a stop and I flew off and into the water. I swam back up to the boat and climbed back in because I was with others and I had help. That was a scary moment for me. I survived that one. It was in the summer, but the water was still cold. I was young and restless and maybe not as careful as I could have been.

Another time I nearly drowned in the river we were on our way to spring camp. I took my older kids. Ted was probably about seven, Sheila five, and Shawna three and it was in the month of April. I was carrying the boat and I slid through the surface of the ice. There were fragments of loose ice around that we call needle ice and as I went through my hip boots filled with needle ice and the weight was pulling me down. It was very hard getting back up on top of the ice and out of the water because of the ice in my boots. My younger brother Bucko helped me. It took quite a while to get me out.

There had been flooding that spring and I was wary of it and I took thirty-five dogs with us to camp. We had plenty of snow. The river provides life, but it takes life, too. I had a few close calls, but I survived. Living here in Akiak it does get dangerous at times. You have to watch yourself at all times traveling on the river and keep an eye on the conditions. You have to be conscious of where you are and what you are doing.

Another time I had a pretty big injury that related to dog mushing. About seventeen years ago, the Williams team was entered in a local village race of about eighteen miles. There was some thawing of the ground alongside the riverbank. It was very late in March and we had a spring carnival with a dog race and there was some open water. Due to the thawing we had to hitch the dogs up and drag them over the riverbank to the snow where it was safer. I took a dog to hitch up to the sled and I was wearing bunny boots, the big rubber boots that are super warm, rather loosely. The dog yanked at me and I slipped on thawed-out wet ground. It had frozen overnight, so it was slick mud and partially frozen. I went down and hit a pile of frozen dirt. The pile was very solid and I twisted my right ankle and heard a big snap.

Initially, I thought I had just sprained it. I tried to walk on it, but the bunny boot was just flopping back and forth. I tried to get up again and I did not have stable footing. I had sprained ankles before playing football and basketball, as many athletes do, so that's why I thought it was just another sprain. Only this time it was broken and every time I tried to stand it wobbled back and forth. A whole crowd of people were watching me because of the spring carnival and I just couldn't get up and walk. I lay down on the mud and couldn't move. The worst part of it was I wasn't even the one racing. I was hooking up the dog for Walter when I got injured.

I just couldn't raise my body to stand on the weak ankle. There were health aides right there. They helped me up the bank of the river and took me to the clinic quickly. When they checked it they thought it was probably broken. But we didn't have a hospital in Akiak. So I had to have a medevac to Bethel. They checked it out in Bethel and immediately made arrangements for me to be flown to Anchorage. There was too much damage. Not only wasn't it a sprain, it wasn't just a simple break. They couldn't do the operation in Bethel. The doctors had to open up the ankle, put some metal in it, and stabilize it. This was starting to become a really big deal.

They took me to the Alaska Native Medical Center in Anchorage, but they could not perform surgery right away. I had to wait a couple of days for the swelling to go down. On my second day in Anchorage, I think, I had the operation. They put in metal screws to put everything back together. Between the swelling going down, the surgery, and the initial healing I was in the hospital for about a week. And all of that resulting from a slight misstep.

The time period of my hospital stay overlapped with April 1, April Fool's Day. A phone call came in for me and the people at the hospital didn't believe that the caller was telling the truth. They thought it was a hoax, or an April Fool's joke. Tony Knowles is a good friend of mine. I think this was after he won the governor's office. I had gotten to know him and his family and he called to see how I was doing. The nurses took the phone call and told me, "Mike Williams, the governor of Alaska is on the phone. Ha, ha. It's probably an April Fool's joke." It really was Governor Knowles and he was very concerned about why I was in the hospital. "What the hell happened, Mike?" he said. I told him how I slipped and how it wasn't a life-threatening situation or anything, but I was stuck in the hospital for a while.

Maggie got on the phone and said, "Hi, Tony." I verified that it was the governor and the medical people in the room still thought it was an April Fool's joke. After the phone call ended they finally believed it was real. Then they suddenly thought they had a special guest as a patient because the governor knows this guy.

The metal is still in my ankle and during some of those cold nights and cold times on the trail it bothers me a little bit. My ankle gets really cold from the metal implanted, though at least I can stand up now.

Another time, during Iditarod signups, Governor Sarah Palin surprised me when she said that I was her hero. She was the sitting governor at the time. Of course, Governor Palin's husband is an avid Iron Dog racer and has competed in that snowmachine race of a thousand miles for many years. Governor Palin was from Wasilla and the June signups and annual picnic were in Wasilla. We were just hanging around and the governor came over. I noticed she had been going around shaking hands with the mushers and everyone was introducing themselves.

When she was coming toward me I said, "Mike Williams" and she said, "Yes, I know." And then she pulled me aside and said that she really appreciated what I was doing by carrying the sobriety pledge signatures in my sled. She said she thought it was great that I was working on that cause and that she appreciated me doing the Iditarod for a good cause. "I've been keeping track of you with what you are doing on the issue of alcohol," she said. "That is pretty commendable. I just want to let you know that you are one of my heroes because of what you stand for. I really support what you are doing."

I was surprised she knew as much about it as she did. Of course, there had been write-ups in the *Anchorage Daily News*. I think that is where she picked it up. But she probably also followed the Iditarod and with her husband racing along the same trail she might have taken a special interest. It can feel pretty good when the governor tells you that you are doing good work.

You know, most of the issues I deal with should not be political. Tony Knowles is a Democrat and Sarah Palin is a Republican. But the issue of suicide should not be political. It does not know any political affiliation, whether you are a member of the Republican Party, the Democratic Party, the Tea Party, the Brown Party, the Red Party, or whatever party. The issue with alcohol knows no race. If a person has a problem, be they black, be they white, be they Asian or Native American, it is a problem that is universal. People become alcoholics and kill themselves and alcohol does not know race.

All of that aside, Governor Knowles was a sympathetic ear to Alaska Native problems. He agreed to hold forums and he issued that executive order recognizing Indian country even if it was a statement from the governor's mansion, not a law. That came about from a yearlong negotiation and it was a public order. We had a good working relationship with Governor Knowles. The gesture by a sitting governor was a good beginning. It is still alive, but it is collecting dust on the state's shelves. As a tribal leader I hoped then and I have always hoped that it would be put into the state statutes.

Dog mushing and being part of the Iditarod has been special to me. It is more than a sport because my participation had so much individual meaning to me. Hunting and fishing are sports to some people, but to us in Akiak they are subsistence activities. But going out to hunt, in particular, has always been a very special time for me.

I always enjoyed hunting in the fall. It started with my father and my older brother Frankie. Later I hunted with my cousins, Sammy Jackson and Bobby Williams. For years we have gone out together hunting moose and camping at the end of August or the first part of September. We go for ten days or two weeks. We have gone as far as Holitna. It is about 150 miles from Akiak up the Kuskokwim River. It takes a day and a half to get there in our boats. We pass Red Devil and Sleetmute. We set up tent camps to sleep in it, tents that are eight by ten. Under hunting regulations we were afforded one bull moose per hunter.

The moose were for Sammy's family, Bobby's family, and my family. I would say that on about 95 percent of our times we could get the moose. I always had a Winchester .270 and I also had a Remington 30.06 model 308 that is a high-powered rifle. We shot them, cut them up, hung them, and smoked them to keep them dry and to keep the maggots out. We traveled in three or four boats because that was a tremendous amount of weight from the meat to take home. Two moose are very heavy on my twenty-three-foot boat.

The moose generally weighed between nine hundred and a thousand pounds or so, so after we cut them up and cleaned them that would be a lot of meat. We also got caribou. We were bringing home enough meat so that our relatives in Akiak would have meat. I really enjoy hunting like that. Those are the best of times. That's one place I don't have a cell phone with me. No cell phone, nothing at all.

In 2001, the three of us were out hunting together like that and it was September 11. That was the day of the terrorist attacks, 9/11, and we noticed some really strange goings-on. We were out hunting in the morning—remember Alaska's time zone is four hours earlier than New York or Washington, D.C.—and there was a whole bunch of military aircraft flying overhead very low. They were going back and forth, though they seemed to be heading toward Anchorage. We starting talking, "What the hell is going on? How come there are so many fighter planes? How come there are so many military aircraft going over us?" That never, ever happened like that. We had no contact with the outside world. We were cut off from what was happening, so we did not know about the terrorist attacks on the World Trade Center, the Pentagon, and the plane in Pennsylvania that crashed.

There were fighter jets and AWACs and then there were no commercial jets because they had been grounded. We just didn't know the news. It was alarming. We thought there was a war or something. We were completely out of touch for a couple of days. It was not until we finished our hunt and were traveling on the river again and stopped at a village that we heard about what happened. We pulled in and people said, "Did you hear what happened in New York? There are a lot of people dead. Everything just stopped. No mail. No flights anywhere." Hunters who were in remote areas—or a few people in similar circumstances—were probably the only people in the whole world who didn't know what was going on with the attacks that day. I heard later that in Alaska when all of the planes were grounded that there were hunters in the backcountry that were supposed to be picked up by planes, but couldn't be. When they allowed the planes to fly again and go get them the flight services were backed up. I heard that they dropped newspapers with the big headlines into some of the camps that they flew over to let the hunters know what had been going on and let them know there would be a delay picking them up.

When my son Ted was young I took him out to hunt for the first time when he was nine or ten. Frankie was still alive and he took Ted out a lot. He really liked Ted and loved taking him. Later, I took Mike Jr. out. The girls didn't go hunting. They stayed home with momma. Junior was eight or nine.

I always enjoyed it when the whole family went to fish camp in the spring. Those were great times with the family camping all together. I hunted geese and birds. Sometimes I went with my friend Willie Lake, too.

I had an uncle named Oscar Kawagley who earned a PhD and when he was writing his doctorate thesis he focused on Native ways of knowing about fish and fish camp. We spent a lot of time talking for three summers. We discussed the science of taking fish and how we ran fish camp,

how we cut the fish, how we preserved the fish, and what it takes to operate a good fish camp. It is not just the fish. It's more than that.

There was mathematics involved in trying to figure out how many
fish we would need to feed the family in the coming months and the art
involved was about the women, my wife, and how they are able to cut the
fish in a way that it will dry properly. It is not just cutting fish, but doing it
the right way.

At the front entrance of the Akiak school there are murals that
depict the Elders of the community. They are not actually paintings, but
taken from photographs and enlarged. There was a guy who does projects
like that throughout the United States who came here to do it. It is not
easy to do, but it is of high quality so the pictures should be up there as
long as the building is standing. That's the kind of quality we looked for.
The sharpness is there and I can tell you stories about the Akiak people in
those pictures.

I am up there and generations of my family are in them. In the picture of me I am holding an ice chipper and it shows my burbot ice trap.
Actually, I think we got 180 lush fish that day. That was a big day and a
successful day. In the mural, some of the people are hunting and some are
fishing. The Elders are symbols of the ancestors and of our old way of life.
My grandpa, great-grandpa, grandmother, and great-grandmother and
some other family members who have passed on are represented there.
That is a mural of part of our Akiak history and of course subsistence
gathering of food is part of that.

The mural reminds us that our ancestors are watching over us and
it shows the children who attend the school part of our history. It dem-
onstrates that those Elders are not forgotten and it shows the skills and
ways they made their lives work that can be reminders to the young people about their culture. They are looking on us to make sure that learning
takes place in this building. That may be hunting, fishing, or other ways.
There are a lot of pictures of fish hanging on drying racks. There are fish
camps pictured. My brother Walter is in the mural with the 1983 Iditarod team.

The school is one building for all grades and the age groups are broken up into wings. We discovered in the design it would be cheaper to

build and easier to provide heat if we made it all one building for the whole school.

It is a very modern school. We have a shop and there is a home economics room and science labs. The library is pretty big and we have a good selection of books. Everything is connected to the Internet. They teach a lot of technology and that is why my grandson Ray and my grandchildren are so savvy about computer systems. They are the ones teaching their parents. I have a long ways to go.

One day I was visiting the school and sitting near the entrance talking and a woman who was going to be a new teacher introduced herself. She said she had heard about Mike Williams and said she heard that I was stubborn and had endurance and passion. It is kind of scary that people you don't know have got all kinds of information about me and it's kind of scary that she knows a lot about me and she just got here. But she was right. None of those three things are wrong. I think she hit those descriptions right, but there is more to me. It's not complete.

Most of the people who follow the Iditarod don't realize how big a job it is. The race may last only 10 days, but you spend the other 355 days preparing for it. After the end of the winter racing season, whether it is the Iditarod or some village races in April, the dogs do get a break. They go on vacation. I like to say that the start of the next racing season begins on August 1. We used to have a business called the Hot Dog Express in Akiak that my cousin ran and on August 1 we hitched up the dogs for the first time, ate hot dogs, and set off fireworks. It became a ritual that we celebrated with hot dogs and fireworks. But Hot Dog Express went out of business.

Summer in Akiak is not like the Lower 48, so it isn't too terribly hot for the dogs. We have a lot of cooler days in August where it is in the forties or fifties. If the dogs are racing that would be too hot for them, but this is the beginning of light workouts and they don't go that far. We start with running the dogs maybe three times a week with them in harness and running attached to a four-wheeler.

On a given day, I will be in the dog yard with Mike Jr., Shawna, Ray, and some of the little ones. As soon as the harnesses come out you can see that the dogs know what is going on and want to run. It is like *Boing!* They spring right up in front of their houses. Much of the time during the summer months the dogs just lie around. But when they see the harnesses and four-wheelers they know we're gonna do something. And they don't want to be left behind.

The dogs just love to run. They love to get out of their doghouses or their dog areas on their chains. It is a relief for them to run and they feel better. It's like a person who exercises. After the first run, which is only a few miles, they are feeling really good and stretched out. The first day we run two ten-dog teams and two twelve-dog teams. Depending on how much help there is in the kennel one team will go and get put away and if there is only one musher that day he will take out the next group. They are only out for twenty-five minutes. Maybe they do three miles. They are good to go again the next day. My son-in-law Gilbert said, "Day one." I said, "Day one and the first of many more."

It probably takes about a week and then they will be really zooming around. The first day is always tough for them. They like a break after twenty-five minutes. It takes them a few runs to get used to it again. They get into shape building muscle, and then by September they're ready to be trained. August is just a stretch-out period. They get up to six or eight miles next. They start to get fit now and from September on they start to get strong for racing.

When my kids come out to the dog yard to help, and they bring their children, it makes it even more fun to work with the dogs. That is one of the things about living in a small place like Akiak. Whenever I am home and my wife is home we never know what members of the family are going to drop in. It could be anyone at any time. They just walk in the door. I love seeing my grandkids even if they run around and wreck the house. When they don't come by for a day, I miss them. I love my grandkids and I think it is great that I can see them all of the time. They are growing up pretty fast. Sometimes they just come by without their parents and stay around for a while. We love having them.

Even if the kids love being around the dogs now you can't tell if they will ever want to run the dogs in a race. Mike Jr. and Gilbert used to run the dogs by leading them on their bicycles with a chain. It was just a bunch of boys with bicycles running pups, maybe one at a time. Four or five boys would have fun taking out a puppy and going two, three, or four miles.

When we were all much younger my cousin Bobby Williams—one of my regular hunting partners—came along. I used to babysit him while his mom and dad were out muskrat trapping. But we sort of grew up together. I really enjoy hunting with Bobby.

Sometimes when we finish hunting and cleaning the moose we are ready and anxious to go home. It might be night and pitch-black on the river, but we don't want to wait. One time it was so dark that you could not see the water, the woods, or any other boats that might be traveling nearby. We carried some little light or a flashlight to know how far apart our boats were. Well, one year we started home in the light, but it got dark on us a hundred miles short of Akiak. We talked about making camp and taking a morning ride home, but we decided we could make it in six or eight more hours. We passed Napaimute, which means "trees" in Yup'ik, and we passed Chuathbaluk, which means "big blueberries." I have a lot of aunts and uncles and cousins there. Then we passed Aniak, which means "to go out."

We exchanged the lead in the boats, led by a little flashlight. I could just see the boat ahead of me with another flashlight. Mostly we just kept traveling even though we could barely see. It would have been easy to crash into a log and tip over, or even run up on the bank. But we were careful. We got home to Akiak at three-thirty in the morning and we were lucky we didn't hit anything floating in the river. We had been gone for fifteen days anyway and we really wanted to get home. That was a trip and a half.

CHAPTER 24

One thing about dog mushing and having a racing kennel is that you are always building a new team. Dogs get old and they are no longer in their racing prime and they have to be replaced, otherwise your whole team slows down. In 2013 one of our dogs, Dancer, became a mother who had a litter of seven pups. When I saw how many pups she had I joked, "A new team." Well, seven dogs practically is a team.

Seven dogs is the minimum for an Iditarod finish. Usually that's what we end up with at the end of the Kusko 300. When you see seven puppies that's why you think that. Dancer is an outstanding dog and I used her in the 2013 Iditarod. I'd rather raise puppies in April, May, or June. August was a little late. Often we give away the females and raise the males, but we decided to raise all of these puppies. That's because Dancer is such a nice dog.

I gave away some other pups to my nephew and other people that wanted to raise a dog. We had one puppy get run over accidentally and it did not survive. Hopefully, Dancer will have good dogs that will become good Iditarod dogs. It really takes a couple of years after they are born to find out.

The dogs will always be a part of my life, even if I never compete in another Iditarod. I want to see Mike Jr. do well and he has been running very well. He has eclipsed what I did racing in the Iditarod and he is just getting started. He has won more prize money and he has had higher finishes. Good for him.

Without training full-time for the Iditarod anymore my focus is more and more on Native issues and problems and what I can do to influence change. If I am supposed to be so influential, as it says in Grossman's book, I want to see change happen that will benefit our people.

The book says, "Mike Williams is part of a larger movement of Americans who have decided to do something about the problems facing their country and the challenges in their personal lives. This movement toward self-reliance and local grass roots activism is becoming an animating force in the culture. Increasingly, Americans have looked to themselves for the answer, not the President, not Congress and they called it 'The New Activism.'"

Well, I have been very involved and I believe in self-determination. That all just fits in with believing in the sovereignty of our tribes. We have been doing those things for thousands of years, long before there was a state government or a federal government. The villages took care of issues at the local level. Carrying the signatures in my sled to Nome that were pledges of sobriety was aimed at getting our leadership to become sober and for everyone to become sober. The state wasn't doing anything on that problem. The federal government wasn't doing anything.

What the book did was highlight people who took matters into their own hands to try to solve problems. I'm not waiting. We should never wait for anybody to come in and deal with our issues. If we know the answer we should go ahead and deal with the issue on the local level. Only in recent times we had to deal with bootleggers in the village. We've seen all of this violence, crimes committed. We don't want to wait around for federal rules to say it is OK to do something about stopping that. We wanted to apply traditional rules right away in Akiak. We had a meeting and decided to go ahead and do it. We chose to try to handle these problems at the local level. We felt if it became unbearable, if people kept bootlegging, we would go ahead and banish them.

We did banish some people from the village. And many other people heard about the sobriety pledge and they pledged to become sober. They acted voluntarily. I think Native nonprofits, Native corporations, and tribal governments have embraced that movement. We did our own signature gathering. We did our own fund-raising. We did not depend on the government to get that rolling.

I had a general idea about the Giraffe award. They want to reward people who stick their neck out and maybe risk ridicule for what they do, or put themselves at financial risk. But I am not willing to say I am one of the heroes. I did joke that I was a hero for a year because that was what I was labeled, but I'm just trying to do common good for our society. I think people should be complimented if they do things like that and be recognized, but I don't need that. I was fortunate to be recognized.

Perhaps the most appalling thing of all going on in rural Alaska is that not every village has running water and flush toilets, that some places still have to use honey buckets to go to the bathroom. Some of the communities are like Third World countries—in the United States. The United States of America is the richest country in the world. It is civilized. How many billions and trillions of dollars have we given out in foreign aid, going to other countries to make them better, for nation-building, while in the backyard here many communities do not have running water. In Akiachak, right near here, half of the village does not have running water. Kwethluk is another village that does not have running water.

The entire United States should be outraged that this is going on. Some villages have potable water. Some have the honey bucket pail system. If you go to Akiachak, just eleven miles from here, you're going to see a honey bucket being hauled right by several houses. A lot of people dump their human waste and everything into that pot. The big pot is picked up every other day, I think, and taken to the lagoon and dumped into it. It smells. And that human waste is spilled along the way. It's a bumpy road where a lot of kids play. They play outdoors and they walk over it.

I know that a lot of people think that running water is no longer an issue in the Alaska Bush, but it still is. It is very true here. After the Alaska Native Claims Settlement Act of 1971 all types of promises were made saying we were going to be uplifted out of Third World conditions.

It was going to change. There was going to be running water, no substandard housing, and roads and electrical systems. If you go to all of the villages, you will see that a lot of them still live in Third World conditions.

There should be a much bigger outcry around the state of Alaska and even around the country that these conditions still exist for Americans. We have tried to gain the attention in the state legislature and in Congress and they say there is no money to fund that. That is impossible. They should be ashamed. Instead, they spend money on other big projects and give money away to other countries. In Akiak we were fortunate that we worked so hard over a lot of years to get state and federal resources together—thanks to the determination of our council— and we have tried to achieve 100 percent running water. In Akiak about 95 percent of the houses are hooked up.

It's all about politics when they say it's too expensive to build the facilities for running water. Any village that is on tundra will have ongoing problems of maintenance because of freeze-ups in the winter. But there's technology out there and there are ways of dealing with these issues. Do we see honey buckets in Anchorage? Do we see honey buckets in Fairbanks? If you have substandard water, health problems grow out of that. You can get hepatitis. It is awful not to have adequate sanitation systems.

The conditions are very hard in our communities and I believe that all contributes to Natives dying younger. It starts with children who grow up in villages that don't have running water. It opens up more risk of disease. I believe in Alaska the Department of Environmental Conservation and the Department of Health and Social Services should be able to resolve that issue. At the federal government level the Bureau of Indian Affairs' Indian Health Service is supposed to provide, but Congress will not fund the sanitation systems and water systems. Compared to the costs of other projects, it is just a drop in the bucket. I think one fighter jet costs about $40 million. I would like to see this country refrain from building just one missile and use the money saved to spend money for plumbing in the Alaska Bush. Look at what we do in foreign affairs. The United States bombs Iraq and then spends money to rebuild it. The United States bombs Afghanistan and then tries to rebuild it. I think using some of this money would be a no-brainer. It starts with adequate housing and then adequate running water systems. We have that brain power. Somehow it seems we are never to be heard. I was just talking to someone today and he was sounding like he was quitting, just giving up. I tried to argue that this is the beginning, not the end. We need to take action right now. We need to deal with them and not give up. He was an older guy and he sounded defeated. Let's not even go there. Let's not even raise that.

It is up to us to educate the outside world and to use the media to let people know what is happening in rural Alaska communities. It is up to us to continuously tell our story. New people are coming to Alaska all of the time, from the Lower 48 and from other parts of the world. They do not know what is happening in rural Alaska. They have no idea what is happening with people in the villages. We also have to make sure that they can tell us apart. They need to learn that there are Yup'ik communities, Aleut communities, Iñupiaq, and Athabascans. We are all different and have to be dealt with differently and individually. The Yup'ik area has its story and the Athabascan community has its story. The Aleuts were uprooted from their home area because of the Japanese invasion during World War II. That's a big story of how they were removed from their homelands. There are so many issues and very little time to tell the stories. If we can continuously tell the stories instead of keeping them within the family, we can make progress. Finally, after listening to me talk, that older guy said that I was right and that we could not quit.

Maybe he just needed somebody to encourage him. We all need that kind of support sometimes. He wanted to hear from somebody who could convince him that there is still hope.

There is a lot of discouragement in Native communities. People say, "Why even raise the issues because they're not going to listen?" "They" are the state government and the federal officials. But I would never sleep if I did not try to do everything I could to see that our issues were addressed. I think the almighty dollar should not rule everything. There is right and wrong and fairness. We are fighting to protect our way of life. Good sanitation is part of good health. In Akiak we are pretty lucky that we have been able to have good water and good sanitation. Everything starts with that. Part of it is dignity. We used to have outhouses and privies and honey buckets. Having running water makes a big difference to health.

It was interesting that recently for about a day and a half we coped without having it because of the repairs at the water plant. That is just a reminder of how challenging life can be when you can't even wash your hands to get them clean when you want to do it.

The shutdown was painful. When we got the water going again in our house it was "Yea! We're clean again." We could wash our hands after we used the bathroom. We could take showers. We could clean ourselves up and wash the dishes and flush the toilet. That is something that you take for granted, but for almost two days we could not do that. When you have something and it is taken away, you miss it. It makes you stop and think what life would be like if you never had it, or you permanently lost it. Losing the running water and the flush toilet for just a couple of days was thought-provoking. When the water came on again it reminded us of how lucky Akiak is compared to some other villages.

I bet people who live in Alabama or Ohio or Idaho don't know that so many Alaska villages do not have running water or full sanitation systems. It probably never crosses their minds that people in a lot of places in Alaska have that problem. This is the twenty-first century. Even if somebody told them I believe that it might be difficult to convince them that this is true and that fellow Americans are living without those modern conveniences because their government will not pay for them.

Certainly, many Americans feel that it is their right to have running water and appropriate sanitation systems. I am sure if they saw the circumstances up close or that somebody told them this was going on, they would be furious. The first thing they would think of is a Third World country. But this is America, the United States, in 2014. I am so angry about this issue and problem. It is horrible that so many Alaska Natives are deprived of these basic services. This is part of the reason that I am an angry man. There is no excuse for a lack of running water, and flush toilets need to be part of everyday life for so many more in rural Alaska.

CHAPTER 25

In the summer of 2014 I was at a fish camp in Akiachak, but the fishing was a struggle because the motor broke on my boat and I was waiting for replacement parts to be shipped in. That's another challenge of living in rural Alaska. When something breaks down you have to send out long distance for parts. We had some nets going catching chum and red salmon for everybody, for the dogs and the humans.

Having an engine break down on the boat shows the difficulties of subsistence hunting and fishing if one piece of the puzzle goes awry. To me, it is all interconnected, just the way our people's problems are connected. You cannot be whole unless everything is working efficiently.

Whether it is climate change, land issues, alcohol abuse, or anything else on the state, national, or international level, we need to bring out how our communities are being impacted. They are all linked together. You know the reason why I am getting involved with climate change: My community is being impacted and I am supposed to stay silent and not try to do anything about it?

Even though it is one more problem it is affecting our communities. If it affects our lives I am going to speak about it. Hopefully there will be a lot of upset people. If I don't do anything to upset people, I'm not doing my job. I'd rather piss off everybody else. Then I'm doing my job.

Most people consider Akiak to be a small place. It has about 350 people and it has always been around the same size during my life. We haven't increased or decreased in population much. Akiak has remained stable. For the last thirty or forty years we have consistently had between 110 and 120 students in the school system.

Generally we have always lived gathering our food, fishing, hunting, picking berries. We gather greens in the spring when they first sprout and we preserve them. It seems like we are always gathering food for winter. Looking at our history that is what we have been doing. We have been living off the land, living off the river, to feed our families every single day.

We catch salmon and dry them and freeze them. We had an agricultural plan to become farmers here, to grow all of our own vegetables in the village. Some missionaries came and some government folks and built these gardens. We have pretty good soil here. We watched them plant potatoes, turnips, and carrots. Families planted gardens and we grew up on vegetables. We almost became farmers, but it did not sustain itself. I don't think we are built to become farmers anyway. We hunt and fish and use what nature provides. We have salmonberries, blackberries, red berries, and blueberries. My wife just picked three gallons of blueberries in Akiachak. We just got through picking salmonberries and in one day we picked forty gallons. We make ice cream out of the blueberries and freeze it.

One thing about Akiak, to some extent you know everybody in the community. And they know me. After all of these years and at my age, sometimes I think I am related to about 98 percent of the community. Except for some folks that came from other villages and married into the community, and some of them are my relatives through marriage. We're also interrelated to other villages in the Yukon River area. I have relatives up north in Kotzebue. That's where some of us originated.

The other day a visiting preacher came to my door and knocked. He was told to seek me out because I am an Elder. I guess I am an Elder.

I'm past sixty years old. At the least I am a senior citizen. It is a huge honor to be considered an Elder and that is a label I do not take lightly. It comes with responsibility. It is a link to a long line of leaders, chiefs in the communities. We have chiefs and leaders and Elders are people who are supposed to lead. I accepted that idea long ago. I spent so much time with the Elders over the last thirty years that I was told, "Mike, we consider you to be part of us, even though you're a young man."

I have spent a lot of time with the Elders over the decades, listening to them, receiving their counsel. I have been studying the Alaska Native Claims Settlement Act and explaining the impact to them. They did not understand it because they could not read or write to understand English words that were legalese. I have spent my time with them explaining the Alaska state constitution, how it is written, and why it was written the way it is. I have explained why tribal governments don't exist in the eyes of the state. I try to explain where we are today and I pick their brains when I talk to them about what life was like before statehood and since then.

There are many questions I have for them about how the communities were governed and what the subsistence policies were. I ask them what they learned from their Elders about first contact with white people and I go back before the Russians or anybody else came. We have compiled that history from them and I wanted to know because that is when our communities were whole.

We used that information to form village councils and to represent the communities. The people decided to organize themselves. Some fifty-six tribes organized themselves in the sixties and seventies. I think the Elders appreciated my attentiveness. I didn't go out and boast or whatever. I just listened and learned and they appreciated that. Sometimes I am asked if my shoulders are wide enough to carry the weight of so much responsibility. I say, no, they are shrinking.

But I believe that there is an answer to every problem. My day starts at six o'clock in the morning and it ends at eleven o'clock at night. I try to end it at ten o'clock in the wintertime. If there are problems on the local level I am going to be on them. I have expended more than half of my life on education issues. When I leave town I am working in another way. I am expending my time as a public servant to carry out the wishes of the people here and while doing that I am raising a family and I have my dog mushing. Sometimes I wonder how I am able to get through the day. But if I do not work on these problems trying to do something about them my day is meaningless. If I know there are problems and I do not try to do something about them, I might be wasting time.

People ask me what I do for fun, but I am having fun working on these issues. I like to talk to people and I like to tell stories and listen to people tell stories. I find time for family and to mush dogs. Mushing dogs counts as fun. But I bring my cell phone to the dog yard. The dog yard is part of my office. I guess I'm on the job all of the time. Thanks to the Internet when I get up early I can get a lot done in the morning. That still allows me time to set fish traps, go fishing, and handle the dogs. I don't have much what you would call goofing off time. It's always work and I am on the move. I don't have time to putter around. I don't have time to be depressed. I don't have time to cause trouble.

The village of Akiak means a lot to me. It is my home and it is where the family is. I want nothing but the best for the community and the quality of life that we can offer to the people. I'll do anything to protect the community. I cannot picture myself living anywhere else. This is home and this is where I am going to be. However, Maggie, who is a teacher, has talked a lot about trying something else, maybe having a teaching position somewhere else before she retires, maybe on the North Slope. She might want to teach for a couple of years in Barrow and then come back here. Or she could take a sabbatical and try something else and maybe I would be going with her. But we would come back here. This is home. We're thinking about building a new house here for me and her. This was our original house, but we feel we can use a brand-new house of our own for retirement and to use to enjoy the rest of our lives.

I can picture that someday I won't work quite so hard. I am just past sixty years old and I have done everything I could do in the short period of my lifetime. My dad lived to be sixty-two and he had a massive heart attack. He didn't really take care of himself physically. He was a chain-smoker and tobacco was his problem. I am getting to be sixty-two and I think about what to do with the rest of my life. I am thinking that when I am sixty-five I want to do something different after that and let all of these responsibilities go to someone of the next generation.

Nobody lives forever and I am not going to either. Some people will not believe that I can let go. I want to do my best to solve problems, but I don't know if everything we're going to be dealing with can be solved in the next few years. There will be skeptics saying, "Mike can't do that. He can't just walk away." Can I just walk away and say I'm going fishing? Or if it is not fishing doing something else I want to do. I don't have a long list of things that I wish I had done, but I would like to go back to South Korea and see where I was in the army and see what it is like now.

It would be fun to see where I was stationed. I also have been interested in Southeast Asia, Japan, and the Philippines, a lot of that part of the world. I have been to Sydney, Australia, Mexico, and to Geneva, Switzerland. I always come back to Akiak. Maggie is always getting on me to exercise more. I have all of these issues to deal with. I am outdoors with the dogs and I walk around all day watering the dogs, feeding the dogs. I do my subsistence activities and they take exercise. I joke that maybe I could use a forty-hour day to do everything. I do think I have to exercise more.

If I stop being involved with all of these commissions and boards and issues at sixty-five I would like to be able to say that my legacy would be that I helped make Akiak a safe community, a good place to raise children, a good place to educate the children and give them a high quality education and that we have been able to stabilize river erosion by mitigating it. I would like to say that we have done something with the quality of housing here and that we have safe drinking water and good sanitation. We have been able to accomplish that here. We have a good infrastructure. I hope my legacy would also be that I've strengthened the tribal community and that we have a sense of protection of our women and children and that we are doing something about the perpetrators of crimes and have a good system to handle those people.

I cannot take any personal pride in these things if they get done because my Elders told me, "Don't let your head swell." But I hope we can embrace a different kind of pride, a pride in our heritage. I want our young people to know who they are with their language intact, with their culture intact, and feel good about who they are. I want them to feel pride in their heritage and to know they have ancestors that were healthy and strong and had a good purpose for living. I want them to know that they have all of these things today and they can continue to live on into the future and preserve all of that and pass it down from generation to generation.

That is the goal of all the work I am putting in—to rise above the bad impacts of the problems we face. I would want to be remembered as someone who helped to overturn that life that was upside down and turned it right-side up. I want to give my grandchildren the quality of life they deserve, and it would be good to know that I did not spend my time in vain for helping provide them with a good future and that I would be thought of as someone who did something to help.

That would be the best reward for the time I have put in and the work I have put in.